THE ULTIMATE

BAKING
FOR ONE
COOKBOOK

175 Super Easy Recipes Made Just for You

Kelly Jaggers

ADAMS MEDIA

NEW YORK LONDON TORONTO SYDNEY NEW DELHI

DEDICATION

To my mother, Carol. I miss you every day.

Adams Media
An Imprint of Simon & Schuster, LLC
100 Technology Center Drive
Stoughton, Massachusetts 02072

First Adams Media trade paperback edition November 2021

ADAMS MEDIA and colophon are trademarks of Simon & Schuster.

For information about special discounts for bulk purchases, please contact Simon & Schuster Special Sales at 1-866-506-1949 or business@simonandschuster.com.

The Simon & Schuster Speakers Bureau can bring authors to your live event. For more information or to book an event contact the Simon & Schuster Speakers Bureau at 1-866-248-3049 or visit our website at www.simonspeakers.com.

Interior design by Sylvia McArdle
Interior images © 123RF/Katsiaryna Pleshakova, chelovector
Photographs by Kelly Jaggers

Manufactured in the United States of America

10 9 8 7 6 5 4 3 2

Library of Congress Cataloging-in-Publication Data
Names: Jaggers, Kelly, author.
Title: The ultimate baking for one cookbook / Kelly Jaggers.
Description: Stoughton, MA: Adams Media, 2021. | Series: Ultimate for one | Includes index.
Identifiers: LCCN 2021032929 | ISBN 9781507217337 (pb) | ISBN 9781507217344 (ebook)
Subjects: LCSH: Baking. | Cooking for one. | LCGFT: Cookbooks.
Classification: LCC TX763 .J34 1996 | DDC 641.8/15--dc23
LC record available at https://lccn.loc.gov/2021032929

ISBN 978-1-5072-1733-7
ISBN 978-1-5072-1734-4 (ebook)

CONTENTS

INTRODUCTION

Baking is the perfect blend of art, science, and pleasure. There's something so gratifying about having a sweet indulgence to treat yourself with when you need it. Unfortunately, most recipes for baked goods seem to make enough to feed a small army! What do you do when you just want a small dessert, but every recipe seems designed for twelve or more? The amount of waste that results can be so daunting that it'll have you reaching for packed, processed foods instead of the home-baked treat you're craving.

The Ultimate Baking for One Cookbook is here to help! In this book, you'll find 175 recipes for your favorite treats and baked goods with all the work of scaling down the portions done for you—so you can have your sweets without all the waste! Want to enjoy a pie just for you? You'll find perfectly portioned recipes like Classic Apple Pie, Pecan Pie, and Silky Chocolate Ganache Tart in Chapter 5. Want a freshly baked cookie or brownie but don't want to have to make three dozen of them? Check out Chapter 2 for Chocolate Chip Cookies, Buttery Sugar Cookies, and Minty Mocha Brownies—all made to satisfy your cravings without all the waste. No matter what you prefer, from sweet treats and decadent desserts to savory breads and buttery biscuits, this book has you covered.

But before you preheat your oven, check out Chapter 1, where you will find the basics of baking for one, baking techniques and terms, lists of tools and pans to make baking for one easier, and ingredients to have on hand so you can bake anytime a craving hits. You will also find troubleshooting tips to give you confidence in the kitchen.

This book will be your guide to a world of delicious baking without waste or worry! Whether you live alone, you're a parent who wants to indulge while the kids enjoy their own treats, or you have a partner who travels, it's always fun to indulge in home-baked treats. Just remember, when you are baking for one, you don't have to share—unless you want to! Enjoy!

CHAPTER 1

BAKING FOR ONE MADE EASY

Baking can be a pleasure. You would be hard-pressed to find many people who don't love a freshly baked cupcake, warm cookies, or a pie with sweet fruit and a crisp, buttery crust. However, recipes for baked goods often make more than a single person can consume, which can lead to food waste or overeating. Fortunately, with recipes made specifically for one person you can still have the pleasure of baking and the satisfaction of a delicious treat, but you don't have to worry about throwing food away or the guilt that often comes with indulging too much.

In this chapter, you will learn basic baking techniques so you will be set up for success. You'll also learn about the tools you need to bake for one, what ingredients are good to have on hand and how to store them, and tips and troubleshooting advice to make your baking successful. With the solid base you learn here, you'll be ready to bake with confidence and to enjoy the perfect portion of whatever you desire! With less waste and more fun, baking for one may become your favorite activity!

TIPS FOR BAKING FOR ONE

Baking just for yourself is much less work and stress than baking a full-batch recipe. It takes far less time overall, and cleanup is generally easier too. Planning ahead and keeping a well-stocked pantry and kitchen will help you to be ready to bake when a craving hits.

Tip 1: Stock Up on Staples

Baked goods generally use a lot of the same ingredients. When you are shopping do not shy away from full-sized bags of flour or sugar, and make sure you have some basic spices like cinnamon and ginger. You can store flour and spices in the refrigerator or freezer to prolong their shelf life.

Tip 2: Try Bulk Shopping

Bulk sections of most grocery stores or natural food stores are a great resource for buying smaller amounts of ingredients for recipes that you might not use up otherwise. Most bulk sections sell dried fruits, nuts, various flours, oats, chocolate, sugar, and sometimes different kinds of candy.

Tip 3: Preparation Is Key

Be sure you check your recipe before you start to bake to make sure you have everything you need so you are not disappointed later. Get out all the bowls, pans, and ingredients before you start baking, and let any ingredients come to room temperature as directed.

Tip 4: Use the Right Size Tools and Bowls

Baking for one will not require your largest bowls and pans. Using the right size bowl will ensure all your ingredients are incorporated properly. The same goes for tools. Smaller whisks and spatulas are better for smaller-batch recipes.

Tip 5: Keep an Eye on It

Watch your small-batch and single-serving baked goods as they bake. Every oven is different, and you can go from perfectly baked to burnt in minutes. Always start checking at the minimum time listed on your recipe, and check every minute until your recipe is baked to your liking.

Tip 6: Get Creative

Measured ingredients like flour, sugar, and leavening are developed in a ratio that makes them successful. It is difficult to make swaps for these ingredients, but you can add your own twist in different ways. First, you can swap granulated sugar for brown sugar in most recipes with little difference in texture. Second, add ingredients like chocolate chips, nuts, and fruits. Feel free to swap or omit them as desired. Finally, try different flavors of extracts. Be sure to reduce the volume of other liquid extracts, such as vanilla, and it's best to use just ⅛ teaspoon of extracts like almond, lemon, butter, peppermint, or fruity extracts like strawberry, banana, and coconut.

BAKING TECHNIQUES

Baking is different from savory cooking in that precision and technique are important. While you may be able to casually toss a little of this and a little of that into your pot of pasta sauce, doing the same with a muffin or cake recipe can lead to disaster. Understanding where you need to adhere to the recipe as written, and where you can add your creative flair, will help you build confidence while baking.

Measuring Dry Ingredients

When measuring any type of flour, you want to employ the scoop-and-sweep method. First, lightly mix your flour so no large clumps are seen. Spoon the flour into your measuring cup until it is slightly heaped. With the blunt side of a butter knife or off-set spatula, gently sweep the excess flour back into the container.

When measuring granulated sugar, it is fine to dip your measuring cup into the sugar directly and scoop it out, but light and dark brown sugar must be packed into the cup to avoid air pockets.

For other dry ingredients such as chocolate, nuts, and fruits, first note if the ingredients are measured whole or chopped. It is best to spoon or gently pack measuring cups with these ingredients. You should scoop leavening agents like baking soda and baking powder directly from the container with the measuring spoon so the contents are heaped, then sweep the excess away with a straight edge.

Measuring Wet Ingredients

Always measure at eye level on a flat surface. Looking level at the measurement lines will ensure you do not under- or over-measure your wet ingredients. When measuring thick, wet ingredients, like sour cream or yogurt, spoon them into the cup and tap it gently as you fill, so the amount is level. If you are measuring sticky ingredients, like molasses or honey, give measuring cups or spoons a quick spritz of nonstick cooking spray to help them release more easily, and to ensure you get the full measure of the ingredient.

Preparing Pans for Baking

The gold standard for preparing cake pans, loaf pans, and cookie sheets is nonstick cooking spray. A light, even coating is enough. If you do not have nonstick spray or prefer not to use it, you can use a light coating of butter or vegetable oil and dust it with a thin layer of flour (or cocoa powder for chocolate cakes). For baking sheets or cake pans, you can use baking parchment, which is a type of paper impregnated with silicone to prevent sticking. You can also use a reusable silicone mat for cookie sheets if you want to cut back on waste.

TOOLS AND EQUIPMENT

A baker is only as good as the tools they use, and baking for one requires more specialized equipment. Never fear, most of this equipment is easy to find at your local home or kitchen stores and can easily be sourced online.

Baking Pans
- ¼ sheet pans
- 6" pie pan
- 8-ounce ramekins
- 4" springform pan
- 4" × 2" round cake pan
- 5" × 3" mini-loaf pan
- 5" × 7" baking dish
- 6" round cake pan
- 8" × 8" cake pan
- 8" loaf pan
- 9" × 5" loaf pan
- Twelve-cup muffin pan
- 4" pie and tart pans
- 6¼" cast iron skillet

Measuring Cups and Spoons
- Dry measuring cups in 1 cup, ½ cup, ⅓ cup, and ¼ cup sizes
- Wet measuring cup with lines for ¼ cup, ⅓ cup, ½ cup, ⅔ cup, ¾ cup, and 1 cup
- Measuring spoons in 1 tablespoon, 1 teaspoon, ½ teaspoon, and ¼ teaspoon sizes

Hand Tools and Knives
- Rubber or silicone heatproof spatula
- Small offset spatula
- Whisk
- Pizza cutter
- Chef's knife
- Paring knife
- Serrated knife

- Strainer or colander
- Fine grater

Small Appliances
- Hand mixer
- Blender
- Food processor

INGREDIENTS AND PANTRY STAPLES

A well-stocked pantry, refrigerator, and freezer will prepare you to be ready to whip up baked treats anytime. The following ingredients will set you up to make many of the recipes in this book and are also useful for other types of cooking and baking.

Refrigerated Ingredients
- Active dry yeast
- Butter, salted and unsalted
- Cheese, shredded
- Cream cheese
- Eggs, large
- Heavy whipping cream
- Jam or jelly
- Maple syrup
- Mayonnaise
- Milk
- Sour cream

Frozen Ingredients
- Frozen fruit
- Puff pastry

Pantry Staples

- All-purpose flour
- Almond extract
- Baking powder
- Baking soda
- Bread flour
- Chocolate chips
- Cornstarch
- Dried fruits
- Dry gelatin
- Granulated sugar
- Honey
- Light brown sugar
- Nonstick cooking spray
- Nut butter
- Nuts—whole or chopped
- Powdered sugar
- Vanilla extract
- Vegetable oil

ADVICE FOR SUCCESS

Experience in baking requires time, effort, and practice. Of course, it helps that you can eat what you make so there is a reward when you are done! This section will offer you tips and advice for successful baking and, in particular, how to bake for one with ease.

How to Read a Recipe

Begin by reading the recipe through at least twice so you are familiar with the ingredients and the order in which they are used. Be on the lookout for divided ingredients that are used in different steps in the recipe. Be sure to note any ingredients or tools that need to be prepped in advance and ingredients that need to be warmed to room temperature before starting; verify oven preheating instructions and pan sizes; and look for any nonactive prep steps like chilling, cooling, or freezing, and see if you can work on any other parts of the recipe during that time. It is always a good idea to verify you have all the ingredients called for before starting and to check that they are fresh and ready to use. There is nothing worse than getting halfway through a recipe and realizing you are out of eggs or butter.

When Is It Done?

Small-batch baking is like any other baking, and you can rely on a good timer as well as your senses to know when your creations are ready. Here are a few things to watch for as the timer ticks down:

- **Look at color:** Most baked goods like cookies and pastry items should be golden to deep brown. Chocolate baked goods, which will be a little trickier, will often have a dull sheen but are not shiny when they are ready. Custards will also have a slightly dull sheen, as will baked cheesecakes.
- **Check the texture:** Cakes, cupcakes, and muffins will spring back when gently pressed in the center, and cakes will pull away from the sides of the pan. Pie and pastry crust will be firm to the touch and flaky. Custards and puddings baked in the oven will be set around the edges but will jiggle slightly in the center.

- **Use your nose:** Once you can smell a baked item, such as cakes, brownies, and cookies, it is almost ready. It is a good practice to peek at your baked items as you near the end of cooking time, and once the smell is strong.

AVOIDING WASTE

Eggs, butter, and milk are no-brainers for refrigerator storage, but other ingredients may also be refrigerated to help them keep longer. Flour, for example, has a pantry life of about six months, but you can extend that to up to a year by stashing your flour in an airtight container in the refrigerator. For even longer storage you can keep your flour in the freezer for up to eighteen months. Other items you can keep in the refrigerator or freezer include chocolate bars and chips, nuts, oats, active dry yeast, maple syrup, and dried fruits.

Just because a baked item is designed for one does not mean you have to finish it all in one sitting. If you have any leftover cookies or brownies, they can be stored at room temperature in an airtight container for up to three days, or frozen for up to a month. Fruit pies can also be kept at room temperature in an airtight container up to two days, along with breads, rolls, and biscuits. Items with dairy, cream cheese, or cheese should be stored in the refrigerator in an airtight container up to three days.

FOOD SAFETY

Before you begin your baking-for-one adventure, please take note of a few food safety tips.

- Never use the same tools for measuring flour to measure other ingredients without washing them in hot, soapy water first, and be sure to avoid putting ready-to-eat baked items on the same surfaces as raw flour. Flour is just ground raw grain, and during harvesting and processing the grains can become contaminated with harmful bacteria, such as pathogenic *Escherichia coli* and *Salmonella*. Flour, like raw eggs and other raw ingredients, should be cooked thoroughly before eating.
- Check ingredients to ensure they are fresh. Oils, nuts and nut butters, flour, and butter should have a pleasant, neutral smell, so a funky or unpleasant smell means it is likely rancid. Same for milk and other dairy products. They should smell slightly sweet in the case of milk and pleasantly tangy for buttermilk, yogurt, and sour cream. Any other odors mean it has spoiled and should be discarded.
- Finally, crack your eggs into a separate bowl. Eggs stored in the refrigerator that are within their best-by date are usually safe to consume, but occasionally an egg may be bad. Rather than ruin other ingredients with a spoiled egg, crack eggs into a small bowl first to check for smell and color.

CHAPTER 2

SMALL-BATCH COOKIES AND BROWNIES

Is there anything better than cookies or brownies warm from the oven? Just the smell of them is enough to make your mouth water! Cookies and brownies are among the most popular sweet treats for a good reason. They are quick to prepare, fun to make, come in a tantalizing array of flavors, and are versatile enough to make a fun snack, yummy breakfast, or decadent dessert. The ultimate in portable comfort food, cookies and brownies are great as an on-the-go treat or tucked into a lunch box to make your work or school lunches a little more special. Is there anything cookies and brownies can't do?

In this chapter you will discover the joys of small-batch cookie and brownie making! The recipes are designed to yield approximately six generously sized cookies or brownies, so there are no worries about cookies going stale before you eat them. From classics like Chocolate Chip Cookies and Classic Cocoa Brownies to more over-the-top creations like Key Lime Butter Cookies, Peanut Butter Crunch Blondies, and Dulce de Leche Blondies, there should be a recipe for every season and every craving. No matter which recipe you choose you are mere moments away from the perfect portion of sweet, rich comfort!

CHOCOLATE CHIP COOKIES

These are no ordinary chocolate chip cookies! Crisp around the edges, tender in the center, and packed with more chocolate chips than should be legal, these cookies are designed to satisfy! If you like, you can use a blend of different baking chips, such as semisweet, white, or milk.

INGREDIENTS

¼ cup salted butter

¼ cup packed light brown sugar

1 tablespoon granulated sugar

1 large egg yolk

¼ teaspoon pure vanilla extract

½ cup all-purpose flour

¼ teaspoon baking soda

¾ cup semisweet chocolate chips

1. Preheat oven to 350°F and line a baking sheet with parchment.

2. In a medium bowl, use a hand mixer on medium speed to cream together butter, brown sugar, and granulated sugar until creamy, about 1 minute. Add egg yolk and vanilla and beat until well combined, about 30 seconds. Scrape down the sides of the bowl as needed.

3. Add flour and baking soda and mix on low speed for 10 seconds to just combine flour, then fold in chocolate chips with a spatula until evenly distributed and no dry flour remains.

4. Scoop dough into six balls and place on prepared baking sheet about 3" apart. Bake 12–14 minutes or until cookies are golden brown around the edges and just set in the center.

5. Cool on the baking sheet 10 minutes before transferring to a wire rack to cool another 10 minutes. Enjoy warm or at room temperature.

Why Salted Butter?

Most traditional recipes for cookies, cakes, and other baked goods call for unsalted butter—because you will season the batter or dough with salt—but in small-batch baking salted butter works better. It is hard to measure an exact "pinch" of salt, but salted butter takes the guesswork out of how much salt to add and helps to ensure the salt is well distributed throughout the dough or batter.

BUTTERY SUGAR COOKIES

PREP TIME: 10 MIN | COOK TIME: 12 MIN | YIELDS 6 COOKIES

These sugar cookies are rich, buttery, and easy to make. You can make these more festive by rolling them in colored sugar for different times of the year. In springtime think pastels, in fall think orange and black, and for the holidays think red and green or blue and white!

INGREDIENTS

¼ cup salted butter, at room temperature

⅓ cup granulated sugar

1 large egg yolk

¼ teaspoon pure vanilla extract

1 drop (about ¹⁄₁₆ teaspoon) almond extract

½ cup all-purpose flour

¼ teaspoon baking powder

⅓ cup coarse decorating sugar

1. Preheat oven to 350°F and line a baking sheet with parchment.

2. In a medium bowl, use a hand mixer on medium speed to cream butter until smooth, about 30 seconds, then add sugar and beat until creamy and lighter in color, about 1 minute. Add egg yolk, vanilla, and almond extract and beat until well combined, about 30 seconds. Scrape down the sides of the bowl as needed.

3. Add flour and baking powder and mix on low speed for 10 seconds to just combine flour, then increase speed to medium and beat until smooth, about 30 seconds.

4. Scoop dough into six balls. Roll each ball in decorating sugar, then place on prepared baking sheet about 1" apart. Bake 12–14 minutes or until cookies are golden brown around the edges and just set in the center.

5. Cool on the baking sheet 10 minutes before transferring to a wire rack to cool to room temperature.

CLASSIC PEANUT BUTTER COOKIES

PREP TIME: 10 MIN | COOK TIME: 8 MIN | YIELDS 6 COOKIES

You can make some fun changes to these cookies to jazz them up if you like. You can swap smooth peanut butter for chunky if you like a nutty bite, or you can add ½ cup of either peanut butter chips or chocolate chips to the dough after the ingredients are just combined. Use a spatula to fold them in, then scoop and bake as directed.

INGREDIENTS

¼ cup salted butter

⅓ cup smooth peanut butter

¼ cup powdered sugar

2 tablespoons packed light brown sugar

½ teaspoon pure vanilla extract

1 large egg yolk

½ cup all-purpose flour

¼ teaspoon baking soda

1. Preheat oven to 350°F and line a baking sheet with parchment.

2. In a medium bowl, use a hand mixer on medium speed to cream butter until smooth, about 30 seconds, then add peanut butter and beat until well mixed, about 30 seconds. Add powdered sugar and brown sugar and beat until creamy and lighter in color, about 1 minute. Add vanilla and egg yolk and beat until well combined, about 30 seconds. Scrape down the sides of the bowl as needed.

3. Add flour and baking soda and mix on low 10 seconds to just combine flour, then increase speed to medium and beat until smooth, about 30 seconds.

4. Scoop dough into six balls and place on prepared baking sheet about 1" apart. With the tines of a fork press each cookie with a crosshatch pattern.

5. Bake 8–10 minutes or until cookies are golden brown around the edges and set in the center.

6. Cool on the baking sheet 10 minutes before transferring to a wire rack to cool to room temperature.

NO-BAKE COOKIES

PREP TIME: 1 HOUR | COOK TIME: 1 MIN | YIELDS 6 COOKIES

No-bake cookies are great on a warm day or anytime you want a cookie without having to turn on your oven. No-bake does not mean no-cook, however. All the cooking is done on the stove, but it takes almost no time. Feel free to add up to ⅓ cup chopped roasted and unsalted peanuts to these for a little more crunch and texture.

INGREDIENTS

⅓ cup granulated sugar

1 tablespoon cocoa powder

2 tablespoons whole milk

1 tablespoon unsalted butter

3 tablespoons creamy peanut butter

⅓ cup plus 1 tablespoon quick-cooking oats

⅛ teaspoon salt

1. Line a baking sheet with wax paper or parchment.

2. In a small saucepan over medium heat, add sugar, cocoa powder, and milk. Bring to a boil and cook 1 minute.

3. Remove pan from heat and stir in remaining ingredients until well combined.

4. Drop mixture into six mounds on prepared baking sheet. Cool to room temperature, then refrigerate 1 hour before serving.

MONSTER COOKIES

PREP TIME: 1 HOUR | COOK TIME: 10 MIN | YIELDS 6 COOKIES

Monster cookies are peanut butter cookies that are packed with goodies such as oats, candy pieces, and chocolate chips. The fun part of monster cookies is that you can add any extras you like, so if candy pieces are not your thing, you can use chopped-up peanut butter cups or candy bars. You can even add a few tablespoons of chopped nuts!

INGREDIENTS

¼ cup salted butter

⅓ cup smooth peanut butter

3 tablespoons granulated sugar

3 tablespoons packed light brown sugar

½ teaspoon pure vanilla extract

1 large egg yolk

½ cup all-purpose flour

¼ teaspoon baking soda

¼ cup old-fashioned oats

¼ cup chocolate-coated candy pieces (such as M&M's)

¼ cup milk chocolate chips

1. Preheat oven to 350°F and line a baking sheet with parchment.

2. In a medium bowl, use a hand mixer on medium speed to cream butter until smooth, about 30 seconds, then add peanut butter and beat until well mixed, about 30 seconds. Add granulated sugar and brown sugar and beat until creamy and lighter in color, about 1 minute. Add vanilla and egg yolk and beat until well combined, about 30 seconds. Scrape down the sides of the bowl as needed.

3. Add flour and baking soda and mix on low 10 seconds to just combine flour. Add oats, candy pieces, and chocolate chips and fold with a spatula to combine.

4. Cover bowl and chill 1 hour.

5. Scoop dough into six balls and place on prepared baking sheet about 1" apart.

6. Bake 10–12 minutes or until cookies are golden brown around the edges and set in the center.

7. Cool on the baking sheet 10 minutes before transferring to a wire rack to cool to room temperature.

OATMEAL RAISIN COOKIES

PREP TIME: 1 HOUR | COOK TIME: 12 MIN | YIELDS 6 COOKIES

You do not need to chill the dough for these cookies, but if you do you will end up with a thicker, chewier, and more flavorful cookie. The chilling time allows the oats to absorb some of the liquid in the dough, helping them to plump before baking. This results in a chewier texture and relaxes the gluten so the edges of the cookie crisp.

INGREDIENTS

¼ cup salted butter

⅓ cup packed light brown sugar

1 large egg yolk

¼ teaspoon pure vanilla extract

½ cup all-purpose flour

¼ teaspoon ground cinnamon

¼ teaspoon baking soda

½ cup old-fashioned oats

¼ cup raisins

1. Preheat oven to 350°F and line a baking sheet with parchment.

2. In a medium bowl, use a hand mixer on medium speed to cream together butter and brown sugar until creamy, about 1 minute. Add egg yolk and vanilla and beat until well combined, about 30 seconds. Scrape down the sides of the bowl as needed.

3. Add flour, cinnamon, and baking soda and mix on low 10 seconds to just combine flour, then fold in oats and raisins with a spatula until evenly distributed and no dry flour remains. Cover the bowl and chill 1 hour.

4. Scoop dough into six balls and place on prepared baking sheet about 1" apart. Bake 12–14 minutes or until cookies are golden brown around the edges and just set in the center.

5. Cool on the baking sheet 10 minutes before transferring to a wire rack to cool another 10 minutes. Enjoy warm or at room temperature.

SNICKERDOODLES

Snickerdoodles originated in New England and are widely popular across the US. The funny name can't be directly tied to any specific origin, but some believe it is a portmanteau of the word *snicker*, meaning "smothered laugh," and *doodle*, a Germanic word meaning "foolish." Whatever the meaning, these Snickerdoodles are delicious!

INGREDIENTS

⅓ cup salted butter

⅓ cup plus 2 tablespoons granulated sugar, divided

1 tablespoon packed light brown sugar

¼ teaspoon pure vanilla extract

1 large egg yolk

¾ cup all-purpose flour

¼ teaspoon baking soda

¼ teaspoon cream of tartar

1 teaspoon ground cinnamon

1. Preheat oven to 350°F and line a baking sheet with parchment.

2. In a medium bowl, use a hand mixer on medium speed to cream together butter, ⅓ cup granulated sugar, and brown sugar until creamy, about 1 minute. Add vanilla and egg yolk and beat until well combined, about 30 seconds. Scrape down the sides of the bowl as needed.

3. Add flour, baking soda, and cream of tartar and mix on low 10 seconds to just combine flour, then increase speed to medium and beat until dough is smooth, about 30 seconds.

4. In a small bowl, combine remaining 2 tablespoons granulated sugar and cinnamon and mix well.

5. Scoop dough into six balls and roll in cinnamon sugar. Place on prepared baking sheet about 1" apart and gently flatten each ball to ½" thick. Bake 9–12 minutes or until cookies are just starting to turn golden brown around the edges.

6. Cool to room temperature on the baking sheet.

GINGERSNAPS

PREP TIME: 1 HOUR | COOK TIME: 10 MIN | YIELDS 6 COOKIES

These cookies get their name from the snappy kick of ginger and from their crisp texture, which comes from using vegetable oil instead of butter. If you have fresh ginger, you can grate up to ¼ teaspoon into the dough to amp up the ginger flavor.

INGREDIENTS

3 tablespoons vegetable oil

¼ cup packed dark brown sugar

1 large egg yolk

½ cup all-purpose flour

¼ teaspoon baking soda

⅛ teaspoon ground cinnamon

⅛ teaspoon ground ginger

1 pinch (about ¹⁄₁₆ teaspoon) cloves

2 tablespoons granulated sugar

1. Preheat oven to 375°F and line a baking sheet with parchment.

2. In a medium bowl, use a hand mixer on medium speed to cream together oil, brown sugar, and egg yolk. Scrape down the sides of the bowl as needed.

3. Add flour, baking soda, cinnamon, ginger, and cloves and mix on low 10 seconds to just combine flour, then increase speed to medium and beat until dough is smooth, about 30 seconds. Cover bowl and chill 1 hour.

4. In a small bowl, add granulated sugar.

5. Scoop dough into six balls and roll in sugar. Place on prepared baking sheet about 2" apart. Bake 10–12 minutes or until cookies are firm in the center.

6. Cool 10 minutes on the baking sheet before transferring to a wire rack to cool to room temperature.

DOUBLE-CHOCOLATE CHUNK COOKIES

PREP TIME: 1 HOUR | COOK TIME: 12 MIN | YIELDS 6 COOKIES

If you do not have chocolate chunks or a chocolate bar to make into chunks, you can use chocolate chips. While the chunks do make for larger pockets of gooey chocolate, chips will certainly do the job. Feel free to add ¼ cup chopped pecans or walnuts to these if you like!

INGREDIENTS

¼ cup salted butter

¼ cup packed light brown sugar

2 tablespoons granulated sugar

1 large egg yolk

½ teaspoon pure vanilla extract

½ cup all-purpose flour

1 tablespoon Dutch-processed cocoa powder

¼ teaspoon baking soda

¾ cup semisweet chocolate chunks

1. Preheat oven to 350°F and line a baking sheet with parchment.

2. In a medium bowl, use a hand mixer on medium speed to cream together butter, brown sugar, and granulated sugar until creamy, about 1 minute. Add egg yolk and vanilla and beat until well combined, about 30 seconds. Scrape down the sides of the bowl as needed.

3. Add flour, cocoa powder, and baking soda and mix on low 10 seconds to just combine flour, then fold in chocolate chunks with a spatula until evenly distributed and no dry flour remains. Cover bowl and chill 1 hour.

4. Scoop dough into six balls and place on prepared baking sheet about 1" apart. Bake 12–14 minutes or until cookies are firm around the edges and just set in the center.

5. Cool on the baking sheet 10 minutes before transferring to a wire rack to cool another 10 minutes. Enjoy warm or at room temperature.

WHITE CHOCOLATE MACADAMIA NUT COOKIES

PREP TIME: 1 HOUR | COOK TIME: 9 MIN | YIELDS 6 COOKIES

There is no need to spend money on premium macadamia nuts for baking. Unless the recipe calls for whole nuts, it is more cost-effective to buy pieces, often called baking pieces. With pieces, there is no need to chop the nuts. You just measure and add to the recipe.

INGREDIENTS

¼ cup salted butter

¼ cup granulated sugar

2 tablespoons packed light brown sugar

¼ teaspoon pure vanilla extract

1 large egg yolk

½ cup all-purpose flour

¼ teaspoon baking soda

⅓ cup white chocolate chips

¼ cup chopped macadamia nuts

1. Preheat oven to 350°F and line a baking sheet with parchment.

2. In a medium bowl, use a hand mixer on medium speed to cream together butter, granulated sugar, and brown sugar until creamy, about 1 minute. Add vanilla and egg yolk and beat until well combined, about 30 seconds. Scrape down the sides of the bowl as needed.

3. Add flour and baking soda and mix on low 10 seconds to just combine flour, then fold in chocolate chips and macadamia nuts with a spatula until evenly distributed and no dry flour remains. Cover bowl and chill 1 hour.

4. Scoop dough into six balls and place on prepared baking sheet about 1" apart. Bake 9–12 minutes or until cookies are golden brown around the edges and just set in the center.

5. Cool on the baking sheet 10 minutes before transferring to a wire rack to cool another 10 minutes. Enjoy warm or at room temperature.

Chilling Cookie Dough
Chilling dough can allow for a few things to happen. First, as the dough chills it dries out, and that results in a chewier cookie with crisper edges. Second, the flavors will have a chance to develop so your cookies will have a more refined flavor. Finally, chilling the dough controls the spread and results in thicker cookies.

PECAN DATE COOKIES

PREP TIME: 1 HOUR | COOK TIME: 8 MIN | YIELDS 6 COOKIES

Dates give these cookies a caramelly sweet flavor and a chewy texture, making them almost irresistible. Chopped dates are available in most stores, but these cookies taste better with freshly chopped dates. The ready-chopped kind are often dry and less flavorful. Any leftover dates can be stashed in the refrigerator and used in smoothies, chopped and added to salads, or used to make more batches of these cookies!

INGREDIENTS

3 tablespoons salted butter

¼ cup granulated sugar

¼ teaspoon pure vanilla extract

1 large egg yolk

½ cup all-purpose flour

⅛ teaspoon baking soda

⅓ cup chopped pecans

¼ cup chopped dates

1. Preheat oven to 350°F and line a baking sheet with parchment.

2. In a medium bowl, use a hand mixer on medium speed to cream together butter and sugar until creamy, about 30 seconds. Add vanilla and egg yolk and beat until well combined, about 30 seconds. Scrape down the sides of the bowl as needed.

3. Add flour and baking soda and mix on low 10 seconds to just combine flour, then fold in pecans and dates with a spatula until evenly distributed and no dry flour remains. Cover bowl and chill 1 hour.

4. Scoop dough into six balls and place on prepared baking sheet about 1" apart. Bake 8–10 minutes or until cookies are golden brown around the edges and just set in the center.

5. Cool on the baking sheet 10 minutes before transferring to a wire rack to cool another 10 minutes. Enjoy warm or at room temperature.

MOLASSES COOKIES

PREP TIME: 1 HOUR | COOK TIME: 9 MIN | YIELDS 6 COOKIES

Molasses makes these cookies soft and chewy and gives them a rich, unique flavor. If you do not have molasses, swap it for honey, and you'll have a soft and chewy honey cookie instead. For a more sparkly cookie, roll them in coarse sanding sugar instead of granulated sugar.

INGREDIENTS

¼ cup salted butter

⅓ cup plus 2 tablespoons granulated sugar, divided

1 tablespoon molasses

1 large egg yolk

½ cup plus 1 tablespoon all-purpose flour

¼ teaspoon baking soda

¼ teaspoon ground cinnamon

⅛ teaspoon ground ginger

⅛ teaspoon pumpkin pie spice

1. Preheat oven to 350°F and line a baking sheet with parchment.

2. In a medium bowl, use a hand mixer on medium speed to cream together butter, ⅓ cup sugar, and molasses until creamy, about 1 minute. Add egg yolk and beat until well combined, about 30 seconds. Scrape down the sides of the bowl as needed.

3. Add flour, baking soda, cinnamon, ginger, and pumpkin pie spice and mix on low 10 seconds to just combine flour, then increase speed to medium and beat until dough is smooth, about 30 seconds. Cover bowl and chill 1 hour.

4. In a small bowl, add remaining 2 tablespoons sugar.

5. Scoop dough into six balls and roll in sugar. Place on prepared baking sheet about 1" apart. Bake 9–12 minutes or until cookies are firm around the edges and set in the center.

6. Cool 10 minutes on the baking sheet before transferring to a wire rack to cool to room temperature.

CHOCOLATE CHIP SKILLET COOKIE

PREP TIME: 10 MIN | COOK TIME: 14 MIN | YIELDS 1 COOKIE

All you need to make this recipe complete is a scoop of your favorite ice cream and a spoon! This makes a BIG cookie and is enough to share if you like. This recipe calls for a 6¼" cast iron skillet, but if you do not have one you can use a 6" round cake pan or even a 6" casserole dish.

INGREDIENTS

3 tablespoons salted butter

2 tablespoons packed light brown sugar

2 tablespoons granulated sugar

1 large egg yolk

¼ teaspoon pure vanilla extract

¼ cup plus 2 tablespoons all-purpose flour

⅛ teaspoon baking soda

⅓ cup semisweet chocolate chips

⅛ teaspoon flaky sea salt

1. Preheat oven to 350°F and lightly grease a 6¼" cast iron skillet with nonstick cooking spray.

2. In a medium bowl, use a hand mixer on medium speed to cream together butter, brown sugar, and granulated sugar until creamy, about 1 minute. Add egg yolk and vanilla and beat until well combined, about 30 seconds. Scrape down the sides of the bowl as needed.

3. Add flour and baking soda and mix on low 10 seconds to just combine flour, then fold in chocolate chips with a spatula until evenly distributed and no dry flour remains.

4. Press cookie dough into prepared skillet in an even layer and sprinkle with sea salt. Bake 14–16 minutes or until cookie is golden brown and puffed around the edges.

5. Remove from oven and cool 10 minutes. Enjoy warm or at room temperature.

BROWN SUGAR PECAN BREAKFAST COOKIES

PREP TIME: 10 MIN | COOK TIME: 14 MIN | YIELDS 6 COOKIES

These nutty breakfast cookies are made even better with a little semisweet chocolate. If you have a bar of good-quality dark chocolate on hand, you can chop it into pieces and use that in place of the chips.

INGREDIENTS

½ cup creamy peanut butter

1 medium banana, peeled and mashed

3 tablespoons packed light brown sugar

½ teaspoon pure vanilla extract

¼ teaspoon sea salt

½ teaspoon ground cinnamon

1 cup quick-cooking oats

½ cup chopped pecans

¼ cup semisweet chocolate chips

1. Preheat oven to 325°F and line a baking sheet with parchment.

2. In a medium bowl, use a hand mixer on medium speed to combine peanut butter, banana, and brown sugar. Beat until well combined, about 30 seconds, then add vanilla, salt, and cinnamon and mix until well combined, about 30 seconds.

3. With a spatula, fold in oats, pecans, and chocolate chips until evenly combined.

4. Scoop dough into six mounds and place on prepared baking sheet 2" apart. Bake 14–16 minutes or until cookies are brown and soft but not gooey. Cool completely on baking sheet.

Freezing Nuts and Chocolate

Freezing nuts and chocolate is an easy way to extend their shelf life and avoid waste if you decide to buy them in bulk. Bulk buying is cost-effective, and using your freezer is a great way to save money and preserve your food. Nuts will keep up to 6 months in an airtight container in the freezer, and chocolate keeps up to 18 months!

KEY LIME BUTTER COOKIES

PREP TIME: 30 MIN | COOK TIME: 12 MIN | YIELDS 6 COOKIES

Let the flavor of these cookies take you away to sandy beaches and blue seas with the tangy flavor of key lime! If you are not able to find key limes in the produce department, you can use regular limes without losing any of the flavor. To make these cookies more festive you can sprinkle the melted white chocolate with green sprinkles before it sets.

INGREDIENTS

¼ cup salted butter, at room temperature

3 tablespoons powdered sugar

1 teaspoon freshly grated key lime zest

¼ teaspoon key lime juice

½ cup all-purpose flour

⅓ cup white chocolate chips

1. Preheat oven to 325°F and line a baking sheet with parchment.

2. In a medium bowl, use a hand mixer on medium speed to cream butter until smooth, about 30 seconds, then add sugar, lime zest, and lime juice and beat until creamy, about 30 seconds. Scrape down the sides of the bowl as needed.

3. Add flour and mix on low 10 seconds to just combine flour, then increase speed to medium and beat until smooth, about 30 seconds. Dough will be firm.

4. Scoop dough into six balls and place on prepared baking sheet 2" apart. With a glass or palm of your hand, flatten each ball to ¼" thickness. Bake 12–14 minutes or until cookies are just golden brown around the bottom edges and just set in the center. Cool on the baking sheet completely to room temperature.

5. In a small microwave-safe bowl, add chocolate chips. Microwave in 15-second intervals, stirring well between each interval, until chocolate is melted. Drizzle or dip cookies with melted chocolate. Place in refrigerator 20 minutes to harden. Bring back to room temperature before serving.

SHORTBREAD COOKIES

PREP TIME: 10 MIN | COOK TIME: 12 MIN | YIELDS 6 COOKIES

Buttery shortbread cookies are perfect with a cup of strong tea or a steaming mug of coffee. If you want to make these special you can drizzle them with a little melted chocolate or sprinkle coarse sanding sugar over the tops before baking for a sparkly top.

INGREDIENTS

¼ cup salted butter, at room temperature

3 tablespoons powdered sugar

1 teaspoon whole milk

¼ teaspoon pure vanilla extract

½ cup all-purpose flour

1. Preheat oven to 325°F and line a baking sheet with parchment.

2. In a medium bowl, use a hand mixer on medium speed to cream butter until smooth, about 30 seconds, then add sugar, milk, and vanilla and beat until creamy, about 30 seconds. Scrape down the sides of the bowl as needed.

3. Add flour and mix on low speed 10 seconds to just combine flour, then increase speed to medium and beat until smooth, about 30 seconds. Dough will be firm.

4. Scoop dough into six balls and place on prepared baking sheet 2" apart. With a glass or palm of your hand, flatten each ball to ¼" thickness. Bake 12–14 minutes or until cookies are just golden brown around the bottom edges and just set in the center. Cool on the baking sheet completely to room temperature.

CLASSIC COCOA BROWNIES

PREP TIME: 10 MIN | COOK TIME: 20 MIN | YIELDS 6 BROWNIES

These brownies are your classic, nostalgic, chocolatey brownie. They are perfect as is, or you can dust them with a little powdered sugar, frost them with Chocolate Buttercream (see Chapter 3), or eat them warm with a scoop of vanilla ice cream.

INGREDIENTS

¼ cup salted butter, at room temperature

¼ cup packed light brown sugar

¼ cup granulated sugar

1 large egg

¾ teaspoon pure vanilla extract

¼ cup all-purpose flour

3 tablespoons Dutch-processed cocoa powder

⅛ teaspoon baking powder

1. Preheat oven to 350°F and spray a 9" × 5" loaf pan with nonstick cooking spray.

2. In a medium bowl, use a hand mixer on medium speed to cream butter until smooth, about 30 seconds. Add brown sugar and granulated sugar and mix on medium speed until well combined, about 30 seconds. Add egg and vanilla and mix on low speed to just combine, about 10 seconds.

3. Sift flour, cocoa powder, and baking powder into bowl and mix on low speed until no dry flour remains, about 20 seconds.

4. Pour batter evenly into prepared pan. Bake 20–24 minutes or until edges are firm and center is just set.

5. Cool in pan 20 minutes, then turn out onto a cutting board and cool 20 minutes more before slicing. Serve warm or at room temperature.

TRIPLE-CHOCOLATE BROWNIES

PREP TIME: 10 MIN | COOK TIME: 20 MIN | YIELDS 6 BROWNIES

If you love chocolate then look no further! These ultra-fudgy brownies are packed with white, milk, and semisweet chocolate chips for a decadent brownie sure to please. If you do not have honey, you can use corn syrup or an additional tablespoon of brown sugar.

INGREDIENTS

¼ cup salted butter, at room temperature

⅓ cup semisweet chocolate chips, divided

¼ cup packed light brown sugar

2 tablespoons granulated sugar

1 tablespoon honey

1 large egg

½ teaspoon pure vanilla extract

¼ cup all-purpose flour

3 tablespoons cocoa powder

¼ cup white chocolate chips

¼ cup milk chocolate chips

1 Preheat oven to 350°F and spray a 9" × 5" loaf pan with nonstick cooking spray, then line pan with parchment, making sure there is an overhang of at least 3".

2 In a medium microwave-safe bowl, combine butter and 2 tablespoons semisweet chocolate chips. Microwave in 30-second intervals, stirring well between each interval, until butter and chocolate are melted.

3 To melted butter and chocolate, add brown sugar, granulated sugar, and honey and mix with a spatula until well combined, about twenty strokes. Add egg and vanilla and beat until egg is thoroughly combined, about thirty strokes.

4 Sift flour and cocoa powder into bowl and gently fold six to eight times until the dry ingredients are just incorporated, then add remaining semisweet chips, white chocolate chips, and milk chocolate chips and fold to combine, about five strokes.

5 Pour batter evenly into prepared pan. Bake 20–24 minutes or until edges are firm and center is just set.

6 Cool in pan 20 minutes, then use excess parchment to lift brownies onto a cutting board. Cool 20 minutes more before slicing. Serve warm or at room temperature.

BLONDIES

PREP TIME: 10 MIN | COOK TIME: 20 MIN | YIELDS 6 BLONDIES

Blondies are not always given the credit they deserve! Aside from being just as rich as their chocolatey siblings, they allow the flavors of vanilla and brown sugar to really sing. If you like, you can fold in up to ⅓ cup chopped nuts, chocolate chips, or candy pieces.

INGREDIENTS

¼ cup salted butter, at room temperature

⅓ cup packed light brown sugar

2 tablespoons granulated sugar

1 large egg yolk

¾ teaspoon pure vanilla extract

⅛ teaspoon almond extract

½ cup all-purpose flour

⅛ teaspoon baking powder

1. Preheat oven to 350°F and spray a 9" × 5" loaf pan with nonstick cooking spray.

2. In a medium bowl, use a hand mixer on medium speed to cream butter until smooth, about 30 seconds. Add brown sugar and granulated sugar and mix on medium speed until well combined, about 30 seconds. Add egg yolk, vanilla, and almond extract and mix on low speed to just combine, about 10 seconds.

3. Sift flour and baking powder into bowl and mix on low speed until no dry flour remains, about 20 seconds.

4. Pour batter evenly into prepared pan. Bake 20–24 minutes or until edges are firm and center is just set.

5. Cool in pan 20 minutes, then turn out onto a cutting board and cool 20 minutes more before slicing. Serve warm or at room temperature.

CHERRY OATMEAL BREAKFAST COOKIES

PREP TIME: 10 MIN | COOK TIME: 14 MIN | YIELDS 6 COOKIES

Cookies for breakfast? Yes, please! These cookies are a fun yet healthy way to start your day. While dried cherries are called for, you can easily swap them for any dried fruits you prefer, or omit the fruit and add more pumpkin seeds or use sunflower seeds instead!

INGREDIENTS

½ cup creamy almond butter

1 medium banana, peeled and mashed

2 tablespoons honey

¾ teaspoon pure vanilla extract

¼ teaspoon sea salt

½ teaspoon pumpkin pie spice

1 cup quick-cooking oats

⅓ cup roughly chopped dried cherries

¼ cup chopped almonds

2 tablespoons unsalted pumpkin seeds

1. Preheat oven to 325°F and line a baking sheet with parchment.

2. In a medium bowl, use a hand mixer on medium speed to combine almond butter, banana, and honey. Beat until well combined, about 30 seconds, then add vanilla, salt, and pumpkin pie spice and mix until well combined, about 30 seconds.

3. With a spatula, fold in oats, cherries, almonds, and pumpkin seeds until evenly combined.

4. Scoop dough into six mounds and place on prepared baking sheet 2" apart. Bake 14–16 minutes or until cookies are brown and soft but not gooey. Cool completely on baking sheet. Enjoy warm or at room temperature.

BROOKIES

PREP TIME: 10 MIN | COOK TIME: 22 MIN | YIELDS 6 BROOKIES

Can't decide between cookies or brownies? With these brookies you do not need to choose. If you have ready-prepared cookie dough from the grocery store, you can swap that here if you like. Two to three pieces, or about ¼ cup, will do the trick.

INGREDIENTS

¼ cup salted butter, at room temperature

⅓ cup semisweet chocolate chips, divided

3 tablespoons packed light brown sugar

3 tablespoons granulated sugar

1 tablespoon honey

1 large egg

½ teaspoon pure vanilla extract

¼ cup all-purpose flour

3 tablespoons Dutch-processed cocoa powder

½ batch Chocolate Chip Cookies dough (see recipe in this chapter)

1. Preheat oven to 350°F and spray a 9" × 5" loaf pan with nonstick cooking spray, then line pan with parchment, making sure there is an overhang of at least 3".

2. In a medium microwave-safe bowl, combine butter and 2 tablespoons chocolate chips. Microwave in 30-second intervals, stirring well between each interval, until butter and chocolate are melted.

3. To melted butter and chocolate, add brown sugar, granulated sugar, and honey and mix with a spatula until well combined, about twenty strokes. Add egg and vanilla and beat until egg is thoroughly combined, about thirty strokes.

4. Sift flour and cocoa powder into bowl and gently fold six to eight times until the dry ingredients are well incorporated, about twelve strokes.

5. Pour batter evenly into prepared pan. Spoon Chocolate Chip Cookies dough evenly onto the brownie batter in heaping teaspoons. Gently press the cookie dough into the batter, then sprinkle reserved chocolate chips over top. Bake 22–26 minutes or until edges are firm and center is just set and the cookie dough pieces are golden.

6. Cool in pan 20 minutes, then use excess parchment to lift Brookies onto a cutting board. Cool 20 minutes more before slicing. Serve warm or at room temperature.

CHEESECAKE BROWNIES

PREP TIME: 10 MIN | COOK TIME: 20 MIN | YIELDS 6 BROWNIES

Tangy cheesecake is a delightful foil to rich brownies, and the swirled effect of these Cheesecake Brownies makes them look as good as they taste! Leftover cream cheese can be used to make Personal Cheesecakes (see Chapter 3) or Peanut Butter Fluff Pie (see Chapter 5).

INGREDIENTS

¼ cup salted butter, at room temperature

¼ cup packed light brown sugar

¼ cup plus 1 tablespoon granulated sugar, divided

1 large egg

1 teaspoon pure vanilla extract, divided

¼ cup all-purpose flour

3 tablespoons Dutch-processed cocoa powder

⅛ teaspoon baking powder

3 ounces cream cheese, at room temperature

1 large egg yolk

1. Preheat oven to 350°F and spray a 9" × 5" loaf pan with nonstick cooking spray.

2. In a medium bowl, use a hand mixer on medium speed to cream butter until smooth, about 30 seconds. Add brown sugar and ¼ cup granulated sugar and mix on medium speed until well combined, about 30 seconds. Add egg and ½ teaspoon vanilla and mix on low speed to just combine, about 10 seconds.

3. Sift flour, cocoa powder, and baking powder into bowl and mix on low speed until no dry flour remains, about 20 seconds. Pour batter evenly into prepared pan.

4. In a separate medium bowl, add remaining 1 tablespoon granulated sugar, remaining ½ teaspoon vanilla, cream cheese, and egg yolk. Beat on medium speed until smooth and creamy, about 1 minute. Pour cheesecake mixture over brownie batter. Use a butter knife to swirl batter so cheesecake and chocolate are swirled to your liking.

5. Bake 20–24 minutes or until edges are firm and center is just set. Cheesecake should not look wet or jiggly.

6. Cool in pan 20 minutes, then turn out onto a cutting board and cool 20 minutes more before slicing. Serve warm or at room temperature.

TURTLE BROWNIES

PREP TIME: 10 MIN | COOK TIME: 20 MIN | YIELDS 6 BROWNIES

When an item is called "turtle" it means it is a combination of chocolate, caramel, and nuts, such as walnuts or pecans.

INGREDIENTS

¼ cup salted butter, at room temperature

½ cup semisweet chocolate chips, divided

¼ cup packed light brown sugar

2 tablespoons granulated sugar

1 tablespoon honey

1 large egg

½ teaspoon pure vanilla extract

¼ cup all-purpose flour

3 tablespoons Dutch-processed cocoa powder

⅓ cup chopped walnuts, divided

6 individually wrapped caramels, such as Kraft Candy Caramels

1½ teaspoons heavy cream

1. Preheat oven to 350°F. Spray a 9" × 5" loaf pan with nonstick cooking spray and then line pan with parchment, making sure there is an overhang of at least 3".

2. In a medium microwave-safe bowl, combine butter and 2 tablespoons chocolate chips. Microwave in 30-second intervals, stirring well between each interval, until butter and chocolate are melted.

3. To melted butter and chocolate, add brown sugar, granulated sugar, and honey and mix with a spatula until well combined, about twenty strokes. Add egg and vanilla and beat until egg is thoroughly combined, about thirty strokes.

4. Sift flour and cocoa powder into bowl and gently fold six to eight times until the dry ingredients are just incorporated, then add ¼ cup chocolate chips and ¼ cup walnuts and fold to combine, about five strokes.

5. Pour batter evenly into prepared pan. Sprinkle remaining chocolate chips and walnuts over top. Bake 20–24 minutes or until edges are firm and center is just set.

6. Cool in pan 20 minutes, then use excess parchment to lift brownies onto a cutting board to cool.

7. In a small microwave-safe bowl, combine caramels and cream. Microwave in 30-second intervals, stirring well between each interval, until caramels are melted. Drizzle melted caramel over warm brownies. Cool to room temperature before serving.

PEANUT BUTTER CRUNCH BLONDIES

PREP TIME: 10 MIN | COOK TIME: 20 MIN | YIELDS 6 BLONDIES

The crunch in these blondies comes from chopped peanuts and candy-coated peanut butter candies. If you are allergic to peanuts feel free to swap almond butter for peanut butter and use your favorite candies and nuts.

INGREDIENTS

¼ cup peanut butter

⅓ cup packed light brown sugar

2 tablespoons granulated sugar

1 large egg

¾ teaspoon pure vanilla extract

½ cup all-purpose flour

⅛ teaspoon baking powder

¼ cup chopped unsalted peanuts

¼ cup candy-coated peanut butter candies, such as Reese's Pieces

1. Preheat oven to 350°F and spray a 9" × 5" loaf pan with nonstick cooking spray.

2. In a medium bowl, use a hand mixer on medium speed to cream peanut butter until smooth, about 30 seconds. Add brown sugar and granulated sugar and mix on medium speed until well combined, about 30 seconds. Add egg and vanilla and mix on low speed to just combine, about 10 seconds.

3. Sift flour and baking powder into bowl and mix on low speed until no dry flour remains, about 20 seconds. Fold in peanuts and peanut butter candies.

4. Pour batter evenly into prepared pan. Bake 20–24 minutes or until edges are firm and center is just set.

5. Cool in pan 20 minutes, then turn out onto a cutting board and cool 20 minutes more before slicing. Serve warm or at room temperature.

COCOA VANILLA SWIRL BROWNIES

PREP TIME: 10 MIN | COOK TIME: 20 MIN | YIELDS 6 BROWNIES

To get the best-looking swirls in these brownies it is important to remember that less is more. The less you swirl, the more definition there will be between the two batters. One or two passes vertically and horizontally in the pan should do the trick!

INGREDIENTS

¼ cup salted butter, at room temperature

⅓ cup packed light brown sugar

2 tablespoons granulated sugar

1 large egg yolk

¾ teaspoon pure vanilla extract

½ cup all-purpose flour

⅛ teaspoon baking powder

2 teaspoons Dutch-processed cocoa powder

½ teaspoon honey

1. Preheat oven to 350°F and spray a 9" × 5" loaf pan with nonstick cooking spray.

2. In a medium bowl, use a hand mixer on medium speed to cream butter until smooth, about 30 seconds. Add brown sugar and granulated sugar and mix on medium speed until well combined, about 30 seconds. Add egg yolk and vanilla and mix on low speed to just combine, about 10 seconds.

3. Sift flour and baking powder into bowl and mix on low speed until no dry flour remains, about 20 seconds.

4. Divide batter evenly between two medium bowls. To one bowl, add cocoa powder and honey and mix well to combine.

5. Pour chocolate batter evenly into prepared pan. Spoon vanilla batter in dollops over chocolate. Use a butter knife to swirl batter so vanilla and chocolate are swirled to your liking. Bake 20–24 minutes or until edges are firm and center is just set.

6. Cool in pan 20 minutes, then turn out onto a cutting board and cool 20 minutes more before slicing. Serve warm or at room temperature.

MINTY MOCHA BROWNIES

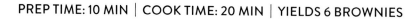

PREP TIME: 10 MIN | COOK TIME: 20 MIN | YIELDS 6 BROWNIES

If you love a peppermint mocha from your favorite coffee shop, then you will love these brownies. Instant coffee powder gives them that mocha kick. Do not freeze or refrigerate leftover instant coffee. Instead, keep it in your pantry in a dark, cool place.

INGREDIENTS

¼ cup salted butter, at room temperature

¼ cup packed light brown sugar

2 tablespoons granulated sugar

2 teaspoons instant coffee

1 large egg

½ teaspoon pure vanilla extract

⅛ teaspoon peppermint extract

¼ cup all-purpose flour

3 tablespoons Dutch-processed cocoa powder

⅛ teaspoon baking powder

1. Preheat oven to 350°F and spray a 9" × 5" loaf pan with nonstick cooking spray.

2. In a medium bowl, use a hand mixer on medium speed to cream butter until smooth, about 30 seconds. Add brown sugar and granulated sugar and mix on medium speed until well combined, about 30 seconds. Add coffee, egg, vanilla, and peppermint extract and mix on low speed to just combine, about 10 seconds.

3. Sift flour, cocoa powder, and baking powder into bowl and mix on low speed until no dry flour remains, about 20 seconds.

4. Pour batter evenly into prepared pan. Bake 20–24 minutes or until edges are firm and center is just set.

5. Cool in pan 20 minutes, then turn out onto a cutting board and cool 20 minutes more before slicing. Serve warm or at room temperature.

Storing Cookies and Brownies

Even with small-batch baking you may have a few cookies or brownies left for the next day. The best way to store them is in an airtight container at room temperature if you plan to eat them within a day or two. For longer storage, you can stash them in the refrigerator up to a week.

FUDGE BROWNIES WITH COFFEE FROSTING

PREP TIME: 10 MIN | COOK TIME: 20 MIN | YIELDS 6 BROWNIES

If you do not have an espresso maker you can use very strong coffee or even instant coffee for the frosting.

INGREDIENTS

¼ cup salted butter, at room temperature

½ cup semisweet chocolate chips, divided

¼ cup packed light brown sugar

2 tablespoons granulated sugar

1 tablespoon honey

1 large egg

½ teaspoon pure vanilla extract

¼ cup all-purpose flour

3 tablespoons cocoa powder

¼ cup chopped pecans

¼ cup unsalted butter

¾ cup powdered sugar

2 tablespoons espresso, cooled to room temperature

⅛ teaspoon salt

1. Preheat oven to 350°F. Spray a 9" × 5" loaf pan with nonstick cooking spray and then line pan with parchment, making sure there is an overhang of at least 3".

2. In a medium microwave-safe bowl, combine salted butter and 2 tablespoons chocolate chips. Microwave in 30-second intervals, stirring well between each interval, until melted.

3. To melted chocolate, add brown sugar, granulated sugar, and honey and mix with a spatula until well combined. Add egg and vanilla and beat until egg is thoroughly combined, about thirty strokes.

4. Sift flour and cocoa powder into bowl and gently fold six to eight times until the dry ingredients are just incorporated, then add remaining chocolate chips and pecans and fold to combine, about five strokes.

5. Pour batter evenly into prepared pan. Bake 20–24 minutes or until edges are firm and center is set.

6. Cool in pan 20 minutes, then use excess parchment to lift brownies onto a cutting board to cool to room temperature.

7. In a small bowl, combine unsalted butter, powdered sugar, espresso, and salt. Beat on low speed for 30 seconds, then increase speed to medium and beat for 1 minute or until well combined and fluffy. Spread frosting over cooled brownies. Serve.

NUTTY BROWNIES

Nuts are rich in antioxidants and fiber, and they are delicious, so adding a variety of nuts to your diet is always a good idea. With this recipe, you can get your nut fix in the form of a fudgy brownie packed with walnuts, pecans, and hazelnuts!

INGREDIENTS

¼ cup salted butter, at room temperature

⅓ cup packed light brown sugar

3 tablespoons granulated sugar

1 teaspoon corn syrup

1 large egg

½ teaspoon pure vanilla extract

¼ cup all-purpose flour

3 tablespoons cocoa powder

⅛ teaspoon baking soda

⅓ cup chopped pecans, divided

⅓ cup chopped walnuts, divided

⅓ cup chopped hazelnuts, divided

1. Preheat oven to 350°F and spray a 9" × 5" loaf pan with nonstick cooking spray.

2. In a medium bowl, use a hand mixer on medium speed to cream butter until smooth, about 30 seconds. Add brown sugar, granulated sugar, and corn syrup and mix on medium speed until well combined, about 30 seconds. Add egg and vanilla and mix on low speed to just combine, about 10 seconds.

3. Sift flour, cocoa powder, and baking soda into bowl and mix on low speed until no dry flour remains, about 20 seconds. Fold in ¼ cup each pecans, walnuts, and hazelnuts until evenly distributed.

4. Pour batter evenly into prepared pan, then sprinkle remaining nuts evenly over top. Bake 20–24 minutes or until edges are firm and center is just set.

5. Cool in pan 20 minutes, then turn out onto a cutting board and cool 20 minutes more before slicing. Serve warm or at room temperature.

ALMOND BUTTER OATMEAL BLONDIES

PREP TIME: 10 MIN | COOK TIME: 20 MIN | YIELDS 6 BLONDIES

Nut butters make an excellent substitute for dairy butter in many recipes while also adding a lovely, nutty taste. If you don't have almond butter on hand, you can make these with peanut butter, sunflower butter, or cashew butter.

INGREDIENTS

¼ cup creamy almond butter

⅓ cup packed light brown sugar

2 tablespoons maple syrup

1 large egg yolk

¾ teaspoon pure vanilla extract

½ cup all-purpose flour

¼ teaspoon ground cinnamon

⅛ teaspoon baking powder

½ cup old-fashioned oats

¼ cup chopped almonds

1. Preheat oven to 350°F and spray a 9" × 5" loaf pan with nonstick cooking spray.

2. In a medium bowl, use a hand mixer on medium speed to cream almond butter until smooth, about 30 seconds. Add brown sugar and maple syrup and mix on medium speed until well combined, about 30 seconds. Add egg yolk and vanilla and mix on low speed to just combine, about 10 seconds.

3. Sift flour, cinnamon, and baking powder into bowl and mix on low speed until no dry flour remains, about 20 seconds. Fold in oats until well combined.

4. Pour batter evenly into prepared pan. Sprinkle top evenly with almonds. Bake 20–24 minutes or until edges are firm and center is just set.

5. Cool in pan 20 minutes, then turn out onto a cutting board and cool 20 minutes more before slicing. Serve warm or at room temperature.

Homemade Nut Butters

If you need a small amount of nut butter for a recipe and you do not want to buy a whole jar, you can make it at home. Simply toast 1½ cups of raw nuts in a dry skillet over medium-low heat until fragrant, about 10 minutes. Let them cool, then add them to a food processor or high-powered blender and process until smooth, 10–12 minutes. You can add a pinch of salt and a little sugar to your nut butter once it is smooth, then let it cool to room temperature and store it in an airtight container in your pantry.

DULCE DE LECHE BLONDIES

PREP TIME: 10 MIN | COOK TIME: 20 MIN | YIELDS 6 BLONDIES

Dulce de leche, which translates to "candy milk" or "sweet milk," is a Latin American treat made by slowly cooking milk and sugar for hours until the mixture is deeply caramelized and thick. You can find it in cans or squeeze tubes in most grocery stores.

INGREDIENTS

¼ cup salted butter, at room temperature

¼ cup packed light brown sugar

3 tablespoons granulated sugar

1 tablespoon honey

1 large egg yolk

¾ teaspoon pure vanilla extract

½ cup all-purpose flour

¼ teaspoon ground cinnamon

⅛ teaspoon baking powder

⅓ cup prepared dulce de leche

1. Preheat oven to 350°F and spray a 9" × 5" loaf pan with nonstick cooking spray.

2. In a medium bowl, use a hand mixer on medium speed to cream butter until smooth, about 30 seconds. Add brown sugar, granulated sugar, and honey and mix on medium speed until well combined, about 30 seconds. Add egg yolk and vanilla and mix on low speed to just combine, about 10 seconds.

3. Sift flour, cinnamon, and baking powder into bowl and mix on low speed until no dry flour remains, about 20 seconds.

4. Pour batter evenly into prepared pan. Dollop dulce de leche over top of batter, then use a butter knife to swirl into batter. Bake 20–24 minutes or until edges are firm and center is just set.

5. Cool in pan 20 minutes, then turn out onto a cutting board and cool 20 minutes more before slicing. Serve warm or at room temperature.

CHAPTER 3
CAKES AND CHEESECAKES

When you think of a celebration, a party, or a gathering of friends and family you probably think of cake. Whether it is a stacked-up layer cake, creamy cheesecake, or a lightning-fast mug cake, cake makes an ordinary day feel special and a rough day feel not so bad. Cakes have a magical, nostalgic quality to them, and when you are eating cake, it is hard to feel bad. The trouble with most cake recipes is they make more than one person could (or should) eat in one sitting. Thankfully, there is a solution!

In this chapter we will explore a variety of individual or small-batch layer cakes, mug cakes, cupcakes, skillet cakes, and cheesecakes. Before you ask, this chapter also has small-batch frosting recipes perfect for one small layer cake or six cupcakes, because what is cake without frosting? Scaled down to make enough for one, these cakes, cupcakes, mug cakes, and cheesecakes are a great way to celebrate, comfort, or simply indulge. With perfectly portioned cakes, any day of the week can be your personal celebration!

CHOCOLATE LAYER CAKE FOR ONE

PREP TIME: 10 MIN | COOK TIME: 18 MIN | YIELDS 1 (4") ROUND LAYER CAKE

Have you ever wanted a whole layer cake for yourself? Now you can have one, and you do not have to share! This cake is very tender and moist and keeps well at room temperature in a covered container for up to three days. If you find you can't finish the whole cake in one sitting, place a little plastic wrap or parchment against the exposed cake to keep it fresh.

INGREDIENTS

⅔ cup all-purpose flour

¼ cup cocoa powder

½ teaspoon baking soda

¼ teaspoon salt

¼ cup vegetable oil

½ cup granulated sugar

1 large egg yolk

2 tablespoons whole milk

½ teaspoon pure vanilla extract

½ cup boiling water

1 Preheat oven to 350°F and spray two 4" × 2" round cake pans with nonstick cooking spray.

2 In a medium bowl, sift together flour, cocoa powder, baking soda, and salt. Set aside.

3 In a small bowl, whisk together oil, sugar, egg yolk, milk, and vanilla. Pour into flour mixture and stir until just combined. Add boiling water in four additions, stirring until smooth after each addition.

4 Divide batter between prepared cake pans. Bake 18–22 minutes or until cakes spring back when gently pressed in center and edges come away from sides of pan.

5 Cool in pans 10 minutes before turning out onto wire racks to cool to room temperature.

6 Once cakes are cooled frost as desired and serve.

Types of Cocoa Powder

There are two main types of cocoa powder. One is unsweetened cocoa powder, or natural cocoa powder. Natural cocoa powder is acidic and works better with baking soda to enhance leavening. With Dutch-processed cocoa powder, the cocoa beans are washed in an alkaline solution to reduce acidity. You should use Dutch-processed cocoa powder in recipes that call for baking powder, as it has an acid included and does not rely on the cocoa powder for that additional boost.

CHOCOLATE BUTTERCREAM

PREP TIME: 10 MIN | COOK TIME: 0 MIN | YIELDS ABOUT 1 CUP

This frosting is a no-cook buttercream, so it is guaranteed to be quick, easy, and luscious. This recipe yields enough frosting for one 4" round layer cake or six cupcakes.

INGREDIENTS

4 tablespoons unsalted butter, at room temperature

1 cup powdered sugar

¼ cup cocoa powder

⅛ teaspoon salt

1 tablespoon whole milk

¼ teaspoon pure vanilla extract

1. In a medium bowl, use a hand mixer on medium speed to cream butter until smooth.

2. Add sugar, cocoa powder, and salt and mix on low speed until just combined, about 30 seconds.

3. Add milk and vanilla and beat on medium speed until smooth and fluffy, about 1 minute.

VANILLA BUTTERCREAM

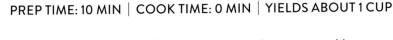

PREP TIME: 10 MIN | COOK TIME: 0 MIN | YIELDS ABOUT 1 CUP

The combination of vanilla extract, almond extract, and butter extract gives this frosting a rich and complex flavor like the frosting from a bakery. This recipe yields enough frosting for one 4" round layer cake or six cupcakes.

INGREDIENTS

4 tablespoons unsalted butter, at room temperature

1 cup powdered sugar

⅛ teaspoon salt

1 tablespoon heavy cream

¼ teaspoon pure vanilla extract

⅛ teaspoon butter-flavored extract

1 drop (about 1/16 teaspoon) almond extract

1. In a medium bowl, use a hand mixer on medium speed to cream butter until smooth.

2. Add sugar and salt to bowl. Mix on low speed until just combined, about 10 seconds.

3. Add cream, vanilla, butter extract, and almond extract. Increase speed to medium and beat until smooth and fluffy, about 1 minute.

GOLDEN BUTTER CAKE FOR ONE

PREP TIME: 10 MIN | COOK TIME: 18 MIN | YIELDS 1 (4") ROUND LAYER CAKE

Butter cake can go from perfectly moist to dry and crumbly in no time, so be sure not to overbake it, or it could turn out dry. Start checking early. The cake is ready when the edges are just pulling back from the sides of the pan and it springs back when you touch the center.

INGREDIENTS

1 cup all-purpose flour

½ teaspoon baking powder

⅛ teaspoon salt

⅔ cup granulated sugar

6 tablespoons unsalted butter, at room temperature

1 large egg

½ teaspoon pure vanilla extract

⅛ teaspoon almond extract

⅓ cup whole milk, at room temperature

1. Preheat oven to 350°F and spray two 4" × 2" round cake pans with nonstick cooking spray.

2. In a medium bowl, sift together flour, baking powder, and salt. Set aside.

3. In a separate medium bowl, add sugar and butter. Use a hand mixer on medium speed to cream until smooth, about 1 minute, then add egg, vanilla, and almond extract and blend until well combined and fluffy, about 1 minute.

4. Add flour mixture to wet ingredients alternately with milk, beating on low speed after each addition until just combined, about 10 seconds.

5. Divide batter between prepared pans. Bake 18–22 minutes or until cakes spring back when gently pressed in center and edges come away from sides of pan. Cool in pans 10 minutes before turning out onto wire racks to cool to room temperature.

6. Once cakes are cooled frost as desired and serve.

MOLTEN CHOCOLATE CAKE

PREP TIME: 10 MIN | COOK TIME: 20 MIN | SERVES 1

Molten Chocolate Cake, with its flowing chocolate center, is easier to make than most people think. It a fun dessert to treat yourself with any time of the day. A scoop of vanilla ice cream or sweetened whipped cream is the perfect accompaniment to this cake.

INGREDIENTS

2 ounces chopped dark chocolate

2 ounces salted butter, at room temperature

1 large egg

2 tablespoons granulated sugar

¼ teaspoon pure vanilla extract

1 tablespoon plus 1 teaspoon all-purpose flour

1. Preheat oven to 350°F. Spray an 8-ounce ramekin with nonstick cooking spray.

2. In the top of a simmering double-boiler, add chocolate. Heat until melted. Remove chocolate from heat and stir in butter until melted. Set aside.

3. In a medium bowl, combine egg and sugar. Use a hand mixer to beat on medium speed until light and fluffy, about 1 minute. Stir in vanilla and chocolate mixture until well combined, then add flour and mix on low speed until no lumps remain, about 30 seconds.

4. Transfer batter to prepared ramekin. Bake 20–25 minutes or until edges of cake are firm and coming away from ramekin but center is soft when gently pressed.

5. Cool cake in ramekin 1 minute before serving. You can serve directly in ramekin or run a thin knife around the edge of the ramekin and carefully turn cake out onto a small plate. Enjoy immediately.

CONFETTI MUG CAKE

PREP TIME: 5 MIN | COOK TIME: 1 MIN | SERVES 1

Need cake in a hurry? A mug cake is the perfect solution. Ready in minutes, a mug cake is the perfect single-serving cake for any time of day or night. Be sure your mug is microwave-safe; otherwise, the handle may become very hot while cooking.

INGREDIENTS

¼ cup all-purpose flour

¼ teaspoon baking powder

1 tablespoon plus 1 teaspoon granulated sugar

3 tablespoons whole milk

1 tablespoon vegetable oil

¼ teaspoon pure vanilla extract

2 tablespoons rainbow sprinkles, divided

2 tablespoons whipped cream

1. In an 8-ounce microwave-safe mug, add flour, baking powder, sugar, milk, oil, and vanilla. Mix with a fork until smooth, then stir in 1½ table-spoons sprinkles.

2. Microwave on high 60–90 seconds or until cake is puffed and cooked through and the top is no longer shiny.

3. Let cake rest in microwave 1 minute, then carefully remove and top with whipped cream and remaining ½ tablespoon sprinkles. Serve immediately.

BOSTON CREAM PIE

PREP TIME: 2¼ HOURS | COOK TIME: 23 MIN | YIELDS 1 (4") ROUND LAYER CAKE

Invented in Boston in the nineteenth century, Bostin Cream Pie is actually a cake made of soft sponge cake layers filled with vanilla custard and topped with chocolate frosting. You can speed up this recipe by swapping the custard for ready-made pudding from the grocery store!

INGREDIENTS

1 cup all-purpose flour

½ teaspoon baking powder

⅛ teaspoon salt

½ cup plus 2 tablespoons granulated sugar, divided

¼ cup vegetable oil

1 large egg

1 teaspoon pure vanilla extract, divided

⅓ cup plus ½ cup whole milk, at room temperature, divided

1 large egg yolk, at room temperature

2 teaspoons cornstarch

1 tablespoon salted butter

2 tablespoons heavy cream

1 tablespoon corn syrup

1 ounce chopped bittersweet chocolate

1. Preheat oven to 350°F and spray two 4" × 2" round cake pans with nonstick cooking spray.

2. In a medium bowl, sift together flour, baking powder, and salt. Set aside.

3. In a separate medium bowl, add ½ cup sugar, oil, egg, and ½ teaspoon vanilla and use a hand mixer to beat on medium speed until well combined, about 1 minute.

4. Add flour mixture alternately with ⅓ cup milk, beating on low speed after each addition until just combined, about 10 seconds.

5. Divide batter between prepared pans. Bake 18–22 minutes or until cakes spring back when gently pressed in center and edges come away from sides of pan. Cool in pans 10 minutes before turning out onto wire racks to cool to room temperature.

6 While cakes cool, prepare filling. In a small sauce-pan over medium heat, warm the remaining ½ cup milk until it just simmers. In a small bowl, whisk 2 tablespoons warm milk into egg yolk to temper, then add to warm milk in pan along with remaining 2 tablespoons sugar and cornstarch. Whisking constantly, bring to a boil, about 4 minutes, and then cook 15 seconds. Turn off heat and whisk in butter and remaining ½ teaspoon vanilla. Transfer custard to a bowl, cover surface of custard with plastic, and refrigerate 2 hours or until well chilled.

7 While custard cools, prepare frosting. In a small saucepan, add cream and corn syrup. Heat until it just simmers, then pour into a heatproof bowl and add chocolate. Let stand 1 minute, then stir until chocolate is melted and frosting is smooth.

8 To assemble, place cake layer top-side down on a large plate. Spread cooled custard over cake, top with second cake top-side down, and spread frosting over top. Serve immediately, or refrigerate up to three days in an airtight container.

CHOCOLATE MUG CAKE

PREP TIME: 5 MIN | COOK TIME: 1 MIN | SERVES 1

The secret to making this Chocolate Mug Cake moist and flavorful is mayonnaise. It replaces oil and egg in this recipe, as well as salt.

INGREDIENTS

3 tablespoons all-purpose flour

3 tablespoons light brown sugar

3 tablespoons Dutch-processed cocoa powder

⅛ teaspoon baking powder

2 tablespoons mayonnaise

2 tablespoons heavy cream

1 tablespoon water

¼ teaspoon pure vanilla extract

1. In an 8-ounce microwave-safe mug, add flour, brown sugar, cocoa powder, and baking powder. Whisk well to combine, then add the remaining ingredients and stir until mixture is smooth. Be careful not to overmix. Use a small spatula to scrape batter from the edges of the mug.

2. Microwave on high 60–90 seconds or until cake rises and center is firm.

3. Cool 30 seconds before removing from microwave and enjoying.

VANILLA MUG CAKE

PREP TIME: 5 MIN | COOK TIME: 1 MIN | SERVES 1

Vanilla beans offer a bright, rich vanilla flavor with a hint of fruitiness. They add a robust vanilla flavor to this quick and easy cake!

INGREDIENTS

1 tablespoon salted butter

¼ cup all-purpose flour

¼ teaspoon baking powder

1 tablespoon plus 1 teaspoon granulated sugar

3 tablespoons whole milk

½ teaspoon vanilla beans scraped from 1 vanilla pod

2 tablespoons whipped cream

1. In an 8-ounce microwave-safe mug, add butter. Microwave on high 20–30 seconds or until melted.

2. To mug, add flour, baking powder, sugar, milk, and vanilla beans. Mix with a fork until smooth.

3. Microwave on high 60–90 seconds or until cake is puffed and the top is no longer shiny.

4. Let cake rest in microwave 1 minute, then remove and top with whipped cream. Serve immediately.

GERMAN CHOCOLATE CUPCAKES

PREP TIME: 30 MIN | COOK TIME: 26 MIN | YIELDS 6 CUPCAKES

The German Chocolate Cake we know today was created in 1852 when baker Samuel German wanted to develop a recipe for his brand of sweet baking chocolate. This interpretation transforms the traditional layer cake into cupcakes!

INGREDIENTS

½ cup all-purpose flour

2 tablespoons cocoa powder

½ teaspoon baking powder

¼ teaspoon baking soda

¼ teaspoon salt

½ cup granulated sugar

3 tablespoons vegetable oil

2 tablespoons sour cream

2 large egg yolks, divided

½ teaspoon pure vanilla extract, divided

½ cup boiling water

¼ cup evaporated milk

¼ cup packed light brown sugar

2 tablespoons salted butter

½ cup shredded sweetened coconut

⅓ cup chopped pecans

1 recipe Chocolate Buttercream (see recipe in this chapter)

1. Preheat oven to 350°F and line six cups of a muffin pan with paper liners.

2. In a medium bowl, sift together flour, cocoa powder, baking powder, baking soda, and salt. Set aside.

3. In a small bowl, whisk together granulated sugar, oil, sour cream, 1 egg yolk, and ¼ teaspoon vanilla. Pour into flour mixture and stir until just combined. Add boiling water in two additions, stirring until smooth after each addition.

4. Divide batter between cupcake liners. Bake 16–18 minutes or until cakes spring back in center when gently pressed. Cool in pans 5 minutes before turning out onto wire racks to cool to room temperature.

5. Next, prepare the coconut pecan topping. In a small saucepan over medium heat, add milk, remaining egg yolk, brown sugar, and butter and mix until egg yolk is completely incorporated. Stir constantly until mixture comes to a boil and thickens, 10–12 minutes. Stir in remaining ¼ teaspoon vanilla, coconut, and pecans. Cool to room temperature.

6. To assemble, pipe a thick ring of Chocolate Buttercream around the edge of each cupcake. Spoon coconut pecan filling into the center. Serve or store cupcakes in the refrigerator in an airtight container up to 3 days.

JAPANESE-STYLE STRAWBERRY CAKE

PREP TIME: 10 MIN | COOK TIME: 18 MIN | YIELDS 1 (4") ROUND LAYER CAKE

This refreshing cake is called "strawberry shortcake" in Japan. It is a popular celebration cake there, and is often served for birthdays and anniversaries and during the holiday season. It is frosted with whipped cream and is best eaten the day it is made.

INGREDIENTS

1 cup all-purpose flour

½ teaspoon baking powder

⅛ teaspoon salt

1 large egg, yolk and white separated

⅔ cup granulated sugar, divided

⅓ cup unsalted butter, at room temperature

¾ teaspoon pure vanilla extract, divided

⅓ cup whole milk, at room temperature

⅓ heavy whipping cream

1 tablespoon powdered sugar

6 medium strawberries, tops removed and cut in half

1. Preheat oven to 350°F and spray two 4" × 2" round cake pans with nonstick cooking spray.

2. In a medium bowl, sift together flour, baking powder, and salt. Set aside.

3. In a separate medium bowl, add egg white. Use a hand mixer to beat on medium speed until frothy, about 20 seconds. While continuing to beat, slowly add 2 tablespoons granulated sugar. Once sugar is added, continue to beat until egg white forms firm peaks, 20–40 seconds. Set aside.

4. In a third medium bowl, use hand mixer on medium speed to cream butter until smooth, then add egg yolk, remaining granulated sugar, and ½ teaspoon vanilla. Beat until well combined and fluffy, about 1 minute.

5. Add flour mixture to wet ingredients alternately with milk, beating on low speed after each addition until just combined, about 10 seconds each. Fold in beaten egg white in two additions, folding until no streaks of egg white remain.

6 Divide batter between prepared pans. Bake 18–22 minutes or until cakes spring back when gently pressed in center and edges come away from sides of pan. Cool in pans 10 minutes before turning out onto wire racks to cool to room temperature.

7 Once cakes are cooled, prepare the filling. In a medium bowl, combine whipping cream, powdered sugar, and remaining ¼ teaspoon vanilla. Use a hand mixer to beat on low speed until sugar is dissolved, about 20 seconds, then beat on medium-high speed until the cream forms soft peaks, about 1 minute.

8 To assemble, place one cake layer top-side down on a large plate. Spread 2 tablespoons whipped cream over cake. Top with 6 strawberry halves, then 2 more tablespoons cream. Place second cake layer top-side down over cream, then frost top of cake with remaining cream. Decorate top with remaining strawberries. Enjoy immediately or refrigerate in an airtight container up to 4 hours.

STRAWBERRY SHORTCAKE

PREP TIME: 10 MIN | COOK TIME: 12 MIN | SERVES 1

This recipe takes the humble strawberry shortcake to the next level! This sweet version adds extra flavor to every bite with a hint of cinnamon and vanilla and a crunchy sugar topping. Fresh strawberries are traditional, but you can make this with blueberries, raspberries, or blackberries. You can even use sliced bananas if you want!

INGREDIENTS

¼ cup plus 1 teaspoon all-purpose flour

¼ teaspoon baking powder

1 teaspoon granulated sugar

⅛ teaspoon ground cinnamon

1 tablespoon cubed salted butter, chilled

2 tablespoons buttermilk

⅛ teaspoon pure vanilla extract

1 teaspoon coarse sanding sugar

½ cup whipped cream

3 medium-sized fresh strawberries, hulled and chopped

1. Preheat oven to 350°F and line a baking sheet with parchment or reusable silicone baking mat.

2. In a medium bowl, combine flour, baking powder, granulated sugar, and cinnamon. Whisk well to combine. Add butter and use your fingers to rub mixture until it resembles coarse sand.

3. Make a well in dry ingredients and add buttermilk and vanilla. Gently stir until a shaggy dough forms and no dry flour remains.

4. Transfer dough onto prepared baking sheet in one heaped mound and sprinkle sanding sugar over top. Bake 12–15 minutes or until biscuit is puffed and golden brown. Cool on the baking sheet 5 minutes before transferring to a large plate.

5. To serve, split biscuit in half horizontally. Spoon ¾ of whipped cream onto bottom biscuit. Sprinkle ¾ of strawberries on cream. Top with biscuit half and garnish with remaining cream and strawberries. Serve immediately.

Tart Strawberries?

If you have berries that are not as sweet as you would like, you can cheat the sweetness by adding ¼ teaspoon sugar for every two chopped or sliced strawberries. The sugar will draw out some of the berries' liquid and will add the sweetness they are missing. Let the berries and sugar stand for 5 minutes, then drain off any excess liquid before using the mixture. This method will make the berries a little softer, but that is a small price to pay for sweet perfection.

CREAM-FILLED CUPCAKES

PREP TIME: 15 MIN | COOK TIME: 16 MIN | YIELDS 6 CUPCAKES

These Cream-Filled Cupcakes are the elevated version of the classic store-bought treat. You can make this filling for any kind of cupcake, and you can even use it to fill sandwich cookies.

INGREDIENTS

½ cup all-purpose flour

2 tablespoons cocoa powder

½ teaspoon baking powder

¼ teaspoon baking soda

⅜ teaspoon salt, divided

½ cup granulated sugar

3 tablespoons vegetable oil

2 tablespoons sour cream

1 large egg yolk

¾ teaspoon pure vanilla extract, divided

½ cup boiling water

1 teaspoon hot water

3.5 ounces (about ½ jar) marshmallow cream

¼ cup vegetable shortening

3 tablespoons powdered sugar

1 recipe Chocolate Buttercream (see recipe in this chapter)

1. Preheat oven to 350°F and line six cups of a muffin pan with paper liners.

2. In a medium bowl, sift together flour, cocoa powder, baking powder, baking soda, and ¼ teaspoon salt. Set aside.

3. In a small bowl, whisk together granulated sugar, oil, sour cream, egg yolk, and ½ teaspoon vanilla. Pour into flour mixture and stir until just combined. Add boiling water in two additions, stirring until smooth after each addition.

4. Divide batter between cupcake liners. Bake 16–18 minutes or until cakes spring back in center when gently pressed. Cool in pans 5 minutes before turning out onto wire racks to cool to room temperature.

5. Next, prepare the cupcake filling. In a medium bowl, combine hot water and remaining ⅛ teaspoon salt. Mix until salt is dissolved, then add remaining ¼ teaspoon vanilla, marshmallow cream, shortening, and powdered sugar and beat on medium speed until mixture is light and fluffy, about 2 minutes. Transfer mixture to a piping bag fitted with a round tip.

6. To assemble, use a paring knife to cut an X into the top of each cupcake. Pipe cream filling into X until it just starts to come out of the top of the cupcake. Frost tops of cupcakes with Chocolate Buttercream. Serve or store cupcakes at room temperature in an airtight container up to 3 days.

STICKY TOFFEE MUG PUDDING

PREP TIME: 5 MIN | COOK TIME: 1 MIN | SERVES 1

You can use ready-chopped dates for this recipe, but you will need to chop them until they are quite fine so they melt into the cake. Adding a small scoop of vanilla ice cream will make this cake more like the versions served in restaurants.

INGREDIENTS

2 medium dates, finely chopped

2 tablespoons boiling water

⅛ teaspoon baking soda

1 tablespoon salted butter, melted

2 tablespoons packed light brown sugar

1 large egg yolk

1 tablespoon plus 2 teaspoons all-purpose flour

⅛ teaspoon baking powder

2 tablespoons caramel sauce

1. In an 8-ounce microwave-safe mug, add dates, water, and baking soda. Stir well, then microwave 30 seconds.

2. To mug, add butter, brown sugar, egg yolk, flour, and baking powder and mix well.

3. Microwave 1 minute 20 seconds or until cake is puffed and cooked through and the top is no longer shiny. Let cake rest in microwave 1 minute before removing.

4. Top with caramel sauce before serving. Enjoy immediately.

PUMPKIN SPICE MUG CAKE

PREP TIME: 5 MIN | COOK TIME: 1 MIN | SERVES 1

Fans of the PSL (Pumpkin Spice Latte) will enjoy this easy-to-make treat! Any leftover pumpkin purée can be refrigerated up to a week and used to make Pumpkin Spice Cheesecake (see recipe in this chapter) and Pumpkin Pie (see Chapter 5).

INGREDIENTS

¼ cup all-purpose flour

¼ teaspoon baking powder

¼ teaspoon pumpkin pie spice

1 tablespoon plus 1 teaspoon granulated sugar

2 tablespoons pumpkin purée

1 tablespoon whole milk

1 tablespoon vegetable oil

¼ teaspoon pure vanilla extract

2 tablespoons whipped cream

1 tablespoon caramel sauce

1. In an 8-ounce microwave-safe mug, add flour, baking powder, pumpkin pie spice, sugar, pumpkin purée, milk, oil, and vanilla. Mix with a fork until smooth.

2. Microwave on high 60–90 seconds or until cake is puffed and cooked through and the top is no longer shiny.

3. Let cake rest in microwave 1 minute, then carefully remove and top with whipped cream and caramel sauce. Serve immediately.

Mug Cake Tips

Here are some tips to help you become a master mug cake maker. First, don't fill your mug more than halfway with batter, or it may spill over while cooking. Second, mug cakes will puff a lot when cooking then sink back down. That is normal and to be expected. Third, mug cakes do not brown, so expect cakes to be pale (unless they are chocolate, of course). Finally, use the lowest cooking time to start, and add time as needed. Your first few cakes may need tweaking, but once you understand your microwave and how it cooks the cakes you will be able to nail the timing.

PERSONAL CHEESECAKES

PREP TIME: 4¼ HOURS | COOK TIME: 26 MIN | YIELDS 6 CHEESECAKES

Ready-crushed graham crackers are available in the baking section of most grocery stores, and leftover crumbs can be kept in the freezer for up to a year. If you have other kinds of crisp cookies, you can use them in place of the graham crackers; just be sure they are finely crushed.

INGREDIENTS

½ cup plus 2 tablespoons graham cracker crumbs

3 tablespoons granulated sugar, divided

3 tablespoons unsalted butter, melted and cooled

4 ounces cream cheese, at room temperature

¼ teaspoon freshly grated lemon zest

¼ teaspoon cornstarch

1 large egg yolk

2 tablespoons sour cream

2 teaspoons heavy cream

¼ teaspoon pure vanilla extract

1. Preheat oven to 350°F and line six cups of a muffin pan with paper liners.

2. In a small bowl, combine cracker crumbs, 1 tablespoon sugar, and butter. Mix until all crumbs are well coated in butter, then divide crumb mixture between prepared muffin cups and press down to form a crust. Bake 8–10 minutes or until crusts are firm, then remove from oven.

3. While crusts are cooling, prepare filling. In a medium bowl, add cream cheese, remaining 2 tablespoons sugar, and lemon zest. Use a hand mixer to beat on medium speed until smooth and creamy, about 2 minutes. Add cornstarch, egg yolk, and sour cream. Beat until well combined, about 30 seconds, then add heavy cream and vanilla and mix on low speed until well incorporated, about 15 seconds.

4. Divide filling between prepared crusts, then gently rap pan on counter three times to level mixture. Bake 18–20 minutes or until cheesecakes are set around edges but centers are still slightly jiggly.

5. Cool in pan to room temperature, then transfer to an airtight container and refrigerate 4 hours before serving.

CHOCOLATE MINI-CHEESECAKES

PREP TIME: 4¼ HOURS | COOK TIME: 26 MIN | YIELDS 6 CHEESECAKES

Using melted chocolate along with cocoa powder will take the chocolate flavor of these mini-cheesecakes to the next level. If you would like to add a little warm spice to these cheesecakes, swap the chocolate cookies for cinnamon graham cracker crumbs in the crust.

INGREDIENTS

½ cup plus 2 tablespoons crushed chocolate cookies

3 tablespoons packed light brown sugar, divided

3 tablespoons unsalted butter, melted and cooled

4 ounces cream cheese, at room temperature

2 tablespoons semisweet chocolate, melted and cooled

1 teaspoon Dutch-processed cocoa powder

¼ teaspoon cornstarch

1 large egg yolk

2 tablespoons sour cream

2 teaspoons heavy cream

¼ teaspoon pure vanilla extract

1. Preheat oven to 350°F and line six cups of a muffin pan with paper liners.

2. In a small bowl, combine cookie crumbs, 1 tablespoon brown sugar, and butter. Mix until all crumbs are well coated in butter, then divide crumb mixture between prepared muffin cups and press down to form a crust. Bake 8–10 minutes or until crusts are firm, then remove from oven.

3. While crusts are cooling, prepare filling. In a medium bowl, add cream cheese, melted chocolate, remaining 2 tablespoons brown sugar, and cocoa powder. Use a hand mixer to beat on medium speed until smooth and creamy, about 2 minutes. Add cornstarch, egg yolk, and sour cream. Beat until well combined, about 30 seconds, then add heavy cream and vanilla and mix on low speed until well incorporated, about 15 seconds.

4. Divide filling between prepared crusts, then gently rap pan on counter three times to level mixture. Bake 18–20 minutes or until cheesecakes are set around edges but centers are still slightly jiggly.

5. Cool in pan to room temperature, then transfer to an airtight container and refrigerate 4 hours before serving.

TEXAS SKILLET SHEET CAKE

PREP TIME: 10 MIN | COOK TIME: 25 MIN | SERVES 1

The origins of this cake are murky at best, but what we do know is that this cake is a staple of potlucks and buffets across Texas and most of America. If you have sour cream on hand, you can substitute it in equal amounts for buttermilk to make the cake even more tender and soft.

INGREDIENTS

¼ cup all-purpose flour

¼ cup granulated sugar

½ teaspoon baking powder

⅛ teaspoon ground cinnamon

4 tablespoons salted butter, divided

5 tablespoons cocoa powder, divided

3 tablespoons water

¼ cup buttermilk

1 large egg

½ teaspoon pure vanilla extract

2 tablespoons whole milk

½ cup powdered sugar

3 tablespoons chopped toasted pecans

1. Preheat oven to 350°F and lightly spray a 6¼" cast iron skillet with nonstick cooking spray.

2. In a medium bowl, add flour, granulated sugar, baking powder, and cinnamon. Whisk to combine, then set aside.

3. In a small saucepan, add 3 tablespoons butter, 3 tablespoons cocoa powder, and water. Heat over medium-low heat, stirring constantly, until butter is melted and cocoa is dissolved, about 5 minutes. Remove from heat and cool slightly, about 3 minutes then add buttermilk, egg, and vanilla and whisk until well combined.

4. Pour wet ingredients into dry and stir until combined, about twelve strokes. Pour batter into prepared skillet and bake 18–22 minutes or until cake springs back when gently pressed in center and edges come away from sides of pan. Remove from oven.

5. While cake cools, prepare frosting. In a small saucepan over medium-low heat, add remaining 1 tablespoon butter, remaining 2 tablespoons cocoa powder, and milk. Once butter has melted and cocoa powder has dissolved, remove from heat and add powdered sugar. Mix until smooth, then add pecans. Pour frosting over warm cake, then allow to cool to room temperature before serving.

LEMON POUND CAKE

PREP TIME: 15 MIN | COOK TIME: 28 MIN | SERVES 1

When it comes to a refreshingly sweet snack to liven up a dull afternoon, you can't go wrong with this tart yet sweet Lemon Pound Cake! Use freshly squeezed lemon juice in the cake and in the glaze for the best flavor.

INGREDIENTS

½ cup all-purpose flour

½ teaspoon baking powder

¼ cup salted butter, at room temperature

½ cup granulated sugar

1 large egg, at room temperature

3½ teaspoons freshly squeezed lemon juice, divided

1 teaspoon freshly grated lemon zest

¼ teaspoon pure vanilla extract

2 tablespoons whole milk

¼ cup powdered sugar

1. Preheat oven to 350°F and spray a 5" × 3" mini-loaf pan with nonstick cooking spray.

2. In a small bowl, add flour and baking powder. Whisk well to incorporate. Set aside.

3. In a medium bowl, add butter and granulated sugar. Use a hand mixer on low speed to cream until sugar is just dissolved, about 10 seconds, then increase speed to medium and beat until light and fluffy, about 2 minutes. Add egg, 2 teaspoons lemon juice, lemon zest, and vanilla and beat until well combined, about 20 seconds.

4. Add flour mixture alternately with milk in three additions, mixing until just combined and no dry flour remains.

5. Transfer batter to prepared pan. Bake 28–30 minutes or until cake springs back when gently pressed in center and edges come away from sides of pan. Cool cake completely in pan before turning out.

6. Once cake is cooled, prepare glaze. In a small bowl, combine remaining 1½ teaspoons lemon juice with powdered sugar and whisk until smooth. Spoon glaze over cooled cake. Serve immediately or cover and store at room temperature up to 3 days.

TURTLE CHEESECAKE

PREP TIME: 2¼ HOURS | COOK TIME: 30 MIN | SERVES 1

Caramel ice cream topping is an easy way to add rich caramel flavor to most desserts like this one, and it will keep in the refrigerator up to a year. If you prefer, you can make the caramel topping by melting three wrapped soft caramels with 1 teaspoon heavy cream in a microwave until smooth.

INGREDIENTS

¼ cup graham cracker crumbs

2 tablespoons granulated sugar, divided

1 tablespoon unsalted butter, melted and cooled

2 ounces cream cheese, at room temperature

¼ teaspoon cornstarch

1 large egg yolk

1 tablespoon sour cream

1 teaspoon heavy cream

¼ teaspoon pure vanilla extract

3 tablespoons caramel sauce

2 tablespoons chopped toasted pecans

2 tablespoons semisweet chocolate, melted

1. Preheat oven to 350°F and spray the bottom of a 4" springform pan with nonstick cooking spray.

2. In a small bowl, combine cracker crumbs, 1 tablespoon sugar, and butter. Mix until all crumbs are well coated in butter, then transfer crumb mixture to prepared pan and press down to form a crust. Bake 8–10 minutes or until crust is firm, then remove from oven.

3. While crust is cooling, prepare filling. In a medium bowl, add cream cheese and remaining 1 tablespoon sugar. Use a hand mixer to beat on medium speed until smooth and creamy, about 2 minutes. Add cornstarch, egg yolk, and sour cream. Beat until well combined, about 30 seconds, then add heavy cream and vanilla and mix on low speed until well incorporated, about 15 seconds.

4. Spread filling onto crust, then gently rap pan on counter three times to level mixture. Bake 22–25 minutes or until cheesecake is set around edges but still slightly jiggly in center. Cool in pan to room temperature, then transfer to an airtight container and refrigerate 2 hours.

5. To assemble, spread caramel sauce over top of cheesecake. Sprinkle pecans over caramel, then drizzle melted chocolate over top. Serve immediately or cover and chill up to 5 days.

CARROT CAKE WITH CREAM CHEESE FROSTING

PREP TIME: 10 MIN | COOK TIME: 18 MIN | YIELDS 1 (4") ROUND LAYER CAKE

The trick to keeping this Carrot Cake extra-moist and tender is swapping vegetable oil for butter.

INGREDIENTS

1 cup all-purpose flour

½ teaspoon baking powder

¾ teaspoon ground cinnamon, divided

⅛ teaspoon ground nutmeg

⅛ teaspoon ground cloves

⅛ teaspoon salt

⅔ cup granulated sugar

6 tablespoons vegetable oil

1 large egg

¾ teaspoon pure vanilla extract, divided

⅓ cup whole milk, at room temperature

¼ cup finely grated carrot

1 ounce cream cheese, at room temperature

2 tablespoons unsalted butter, at room temperature

½ cup powdered sugar

1. Preheat oven to 350°F and spray two 4" × 2" round cake pans with nonstick cooking spray.

2. In a medium bowl, sift together flour, baking powder, ½ teaspoon cinnamon, nutmeg, cloves, and salt. Set aside.

3. In a large bowl, add granulated sugar, oil, egg, and ½ teaspoon vanilla. Use a hand mixer to blend on low speed until well combined, about 1 minute.

4. Add flour mixture alternately with milk, beating on low speed after each addition until just combined, about 10 seconds per addition. Fold in grated carrot.

5. Divide batter between prepared pans. Bake 18–22 minutes or until cakes spring back when gently pressed in center and edges come away from sides of pan. Cool in pans 10 minutes before turning out onto wire racks to cool to room temperature.

6. Once cakes are cooled, prepare frosting. In a medium bowl, combine cream cheese and butter. Use a hand mixer to beat on low speed until smooth, about 1 minute. Add powdered sugar, remaining cinnamon, and remaining vanilla and beat until smooth and fluffy, about 1 minute.

7. To assemble, place one cake layer top-side down on a large plate. Add half of frosting and spread in an even layer. Top with second cake layer top-side down and spread remaining frosting over top. Enjoy immediately or refrigerate up to 3 days.

VANILLA BEAN CHEESECAKE WITH CHERRY TOPPING

PREP TIME: 4¼ HOURS | COOK TIME: 33 MIN | SERVES 1

Dark sweet cherries are available in the freezer section year-round and are always sweet and tasty.

INGREDIENTS

¼ cup vanilla wafer cookie crumbs

2 tablespoons granulated sugar, divided

1 tablespoon unsalted butter, melted and cooled

2 ounces cream cheese, at room temperature

¼ teaspoon cornstarch

1 large egg yolk

1 tablespoon sour cream

1 teaspoon heavy cream

¼ teaspoon vanilla bean paste

¼ cup frozen chopped dark sweet cherries, thawed

1 tablespoon powdered sugar

⅛ teaspoon almond extract

1. Preheat oven to 350°F and spray the bottom of a 4" springform pan with nonstick cooking spray.

2. In a small bowl, combine vanilla wafer crumbs, 1 tablespoon granulated sugar, and butter. Mix until all crumbs are well coated in butter, then transfer crumb mixture to prepared pan and press down to form a crust. Bake 8–10 minutes or until crust is firm, then remove from oven.

3. While crust is cooling, prepare filling. In a medium bowl, add cream cheese and remaining 1 tablespoon sugar. Use a hand mixer to beat on medium speed until smooth and creamy, about 2 minutes. Add cornstarch, egg yolk, and sour cream. Beat until well combined, about 30 seconds, then add heavy cream and vanilla bean paste and mix on low speed until well incorporated, about 15 seconds.

4. Spread filling onto crust, then gently rap pan on counter three times to level mixture. Bake 22–25 minutes or until cheesecake is set around edges but still slightly jiggly in center. Cool in pan, then put in an airtight container and refrigerate 2 hours.

5. To prepare the topping, in a small saucepan over medium-low heat, add cherries and powdered sugar. Bring to a simmer, about 2 minutes, then reduce heat to low and cook, stirring constantly, until cherries are thick, about 1 minute. Remove from heat and stir in almond extract. Cool completely before spooning over cheesecake. Serve immediately.

BUTTER RUM MUG CAKE

PREP TIME: 5 MIN | COOK TIME: 3 MIN | SERVES 1

If you prefer not to use rum or do not have it, you can stir in ⅛ teaspoon of rum extract after melting the butter and brown sugar, or you can leave it out and add an additional ⅛ teaspoon of vanilla.

INGREDIENTS

1 tablespoon salted butter

1 teaspoon dark rum

1 tablespoon plus 3 teaspoons packed light brown sugar, divided

¼ cup all-purpose flour

¼ teaspoon baking powder

3 tablespoons whole milk

1 tablespoon vegetable oil

¼ teaspoon pure vanilla extract

1. In a small microwave-safe bowl, combine butter, rum, and 2 teaspoons brown sugar. Microwave 30 seconds, stir, then heat for 15-second bursts until butter is melted and bubbling and sugar is dissolved. Set aside.

2. In an 8-ounce microwave-safe mug, add flour, baking powder, remaining 1 tablespoon plus 1 teaspoon brown sugar, milk, oil, and vanilla. Mix with a fork until smooth.

3. Microwave on high 60–90 seconds or until cake is puffed and cooked through and the top is no longer shiny.

4. Let cake rest in microwave 1 minute, then carefully remove. With a toothpick poke a few holes into cake, then pour butter rum mixture over it. Serve immediately.

PUMPKIN SPICE CHEESECAKE

PREP TIME: 4¼ HOURS | COOK TIME: 30 MIN | SERVES 1

This cheesecake is delicious all on its own, but if you want to add a little extra decadence you can top it with sweetened whipped cream, dust with a sprinkle of ground cinnamon, and drizzle all of that with a tablespoon of caramel sauce. A few chopped and toasted pecans would also be nice!

INGREDIENTS

¼ cup cinnamon graham cracker crumbs

1 tablespoon granulated sugar

1 tablespoon unsalted butter, melted and cooled

2 ounces cream cheese, at room temperature

2 tablespoons pumpkin purée

1 tablespoon packed light brown sugar

¼ teaspoon cornstarch

¼ teaspoon pumpkin pie spice

1 large egg yolk

1 tablespoon sour cream

1 teaspoon heavy cream

¼ teaspoon pure vanilla extract

1. Preheat oven to 350°F and spray the bottom of a 4" springform pan with nonstick cooking spray.

2. In a small bowl, combine cracker crumbs, granulated sugar, and butter. Mix until all crumbs are well coated in butter, then transfer crumb mixture into prepared pan and press down to form a crust. Bake 8–10 minutes or until crust is firm, then remove from oven.

3. While crust is cooling, prepare filling. In a medium bowl, add cream cheese, pumpkin purée, and brown sugar. Use a hand mixer to beat on medium speed until smooth and creamy, about 2 minutes. Add cornstarch, pumpkin pie spice, egg yolk, and sour cream. Beat until well combined, about 30 seconds. Add heavy cream and vanilla and mix on low speed until well incorporated, about 15 seconds.

4. Spread filling onto crust, then gently rap pan on counter three times to level mixture. Bake 22–25 minutes or until cheesecake is set around edges but still slightly jiggly in center. Cool in pan to room temperature, then transfer to an airtight container and refrigerate 2 hours before serving.

COCONUT MUG CAKE

PREP TIME: 5 MIN | COOK TIME: 1 MIN | SERVES 1

The southern holiday classic coconut cake is made quick, easy, and perfectly portioned in this mug cake adaptation. For a toasted coconut version, place coconut in a dry skillet over medium-low heat. Cook, stirring constantly, until golden brown, 5–8 minutes.

INGREDIENTS

¼ cup all-purpose flour

3 tablespoons shredded sweetened coconut, divided

1 tablespoon plus 2 teaspoons granulated sugar

¼ teaspoon baking powder

3 tablespoons whole milk

1 tablespoon vegetable oil

⅛ teaspoon pure vanilla extract

⅛ teaspoon coconut extract

2 tablespoons whipped cream

1. In an 8-ounce microwave-safe mug, add flour, 2 tablespoons coconut, sugar, baking powder, milk, oil, vanilla, and coconut extract. Mix with a fork until smooth.

2. Microwave on high 60–90 seconds or until cake is puffed and cooked through and the top is no longer shiny.

3. Let cake rest in microwave 1 minute, then carefully remove and top with whipped cream and remaining 1 tablespoon coconut. Serve immediately.

MINTY MINI-CHEESECAKES

PREP TIME: 4¼ HOURS | COOK TIME: 26 MIN | YIELDS 6 CHEESECAKES

Crushed crème de menthe candy is available around the holidays in most grocery stores, but if you can't find it, you can roughly chop whole crème de menthe candies.

INGREDIENTS

½ cup plus 2 tablespoons chocolate cookie crumbs

3 tablespoons granulated sugar, divided

3 tablespoons unsalted butter, melted and cooled

4 ounces cream cheese, at room temperature

1 tablespoon crème de menthe liqueur or ¼ teaspoon mint extract

¼ teaspoon cornstarch

1 large egg yolk

2 tablespoons sour cream

2 teaspoons heavy cream

¼ teaspoon pure vanilla extract

⅔ cup crème de menthe candy bits, divided

1. Preheat oven to 350°F and line six cups of a muffin pan with paper liners.

2. In a small bowl, combine cookie crumbs, 1 tablespoon sugar, and butter. Mix until all crumbs are well coated in butter, then divide crumb mixture between prepared muffin cups and press down to form a crust. Bake 8–10 minutes or until crusts are firm, then remove from oven.

3. While crusts are cooling, prepare filling. In a medium bowl, add cream cheese, crème de menthe liqueur or mint extract, and remaining 2 tablespoons sugar. Beat on medium speed until smooth and creamy, about 2 minutes. Add cornstarch, egg yolk, and sour cream. Beat until well combined, about 30 seconds. Add heavy cream and vanilla and mix on low speed until well incorporated, about 15 seconds. Fold in ½ cup crème de menthe candy pieces.

4. Divide filling between prepared crusts, then gently rap pan on counter three times to level mixture. Sprinkle remaining crème de menthe candy pieces on tops of cheesecakes. Bake 18–20 minutes or until cheesecakes are set around edges but still slightly jiggly in centers. Cool in pan to room temperature, then transfer to an airtight container and refrigerate 4 hours before serving.

CHOCOLATE COCONUT CUPCAKES

PREP TIME: 30 MIN | COOK TIME: 16 MIN | YIELDS 6 CUPCAKES

Chocolate and coconut are a delicious combination, and when you add luscious Vanilla Buttercream (see recipe in this chapter) to the mix you have a cupcake that coconut lovers will swoon for.

INGREDIENTS

½ cup all-purpose flour

2 tablespoons Dutch-processed cocoa powder

½ teaspoon baking powder

¼ teaspoon baking soda

¼ teaspoon salt

½ cup granulated sugar

3 tablespoons melted butter

¼ cup sour cream

1 large egg yolk

½ teaspoon pure vanilla extract

⅛ teaspoon coconut extract

¼ cup boiling water

½ cup shredded sweetened coconut

1 recipe Vanilla Buttercream (see recipe in this chapter)

1. Preheat oven to 350°F and line six cups of a muffin pan with paper liners.

2. In a medium bowl, sift together flour, cocoa powder, baking powder, baking soda, and salt. Set aside.

3. In a small bowl, whisk together sugar, butter, sour cream, egg yolk, vanilla, and coconut extract. Pour into flour mixture and stir until just combined. Add boiling water, stirring until smooth. Fold in shredded coconut.

4. Divide batter between cupcake liners. Bake 16–18 minutes or until cakes spring back in center when gently pressed. Cool in pans 5 minutes before turning out onto wire racks to cool to room temperature.

5. To assemble, frost each cupcake with Vanilla Buttercream. Store cupcakes in the refrigerator in an airtight container up to 3 days.

JELLY ROLL FOR ONE

PREP TIME: 10 MIN | COOK TIME: 8 MIN | SERVES 1

A jelly roll may seem complex, but it is really about timing. The cake must be hot when you roll it the first time to avoid cracks. If you prefer to avoid that step, cook the cake on a wire rack, cut it in half, spread the jelly on one half, top it with the second half, and enjoy!

INGREDIENTS

3 tablespoons powdered sugar, divided

¼ cup all-purpose flour

¼ teaspoon baking powder

1 large egg

⅓ cup granulated sugar

1 tablespoon water

¼ teaspoon pure vanilla extract

3 tablespoons seedless raspberry jam

1. Preheat oven to 375°F and spray a 9" × 5" loaf pan with nonstick cooking spray. Line pan with strips of parchment, allowing paper to hang over sides of pan. Spray parchment lightly with nonstick cooking spray.

2. Sprinkle a clean towel with 2 tablespoons powdered sugar. Set aside.

3. In a small bowl, sift together flour and baking powder. Set aside.

4. In a medium bowl, use a hand mixer to beat egg on high speed for 3 minutes or until pale yellow and thick. Gradually beat in granulated sugar until egg forms a ribbon when beaters are lifted from the mixture that takes a second to flatten out.

5. Reduce speed to low and beat in water and vanilla, then add flour mixture in three additions, mixing until batter is smooth between each addition.

6. Spread batter in prepared pan. Bake 8–10 minutes or until cake springs back when gently pressed in center and edges come away from sides of pan.

7. Using parchment remove cake from pan and turn out onto prepared towel. While cake is hot roll cake in towel from narrow end. Cool on a wire rack to room temperature.

8. Once cool, carefully unroll cake. Spread jam onto cake and roll up cake. Sprinkle top with remaining 1 tablespoon powdered sugar.

CRANBERRY COFFEE CAKE

PREP TIME: 10 MIN | COOK TIME: 18 MIN | SERVES 1

Cranberry Coffee Cake is the perfect treat to use up cranberry sauce around the holidays. It goes well with a cup of hot coffee or a mug of black tea. This cake uses whole-berry cranberry sauce from a can, but you can swap it for jellied cranberry sauce. You can also eliminate the cranberry sauce in place of any jam you like, so feel free to experiment!

INGREDIENTS

½ cup all-purpose flour

¼ teaspoon baking powder

¼ cup salted butter, at room temperature

¼ cup granulated sugar

1 large egg white

½ teaspoon pure vanilla extract

⅛ teaspoon almond extract

2 tablespoons sour cream

¼ cup chopped walnuts, divided

⅓ cup whole-berry cranberry sauce

1. Preheat oven to 350°F and spray a 6¼" cast iron skillet with nonstick cooking spray.

2. In a medium bowl, sift together flour and baking powder. Set aside.

3. In a separate medium bowl, add butter and sugar. Use a hand mixer on medium speed to cream until smooth, about 1 minute, then add egg white, vanilla, and almond extract and blend until well combined and fluffy, about 1 minute.

4. Add flour mixture alternately with sour cream, beating on low speed for 10 seconds after each addition until just combined.

5. Add half of batter to pan and spread until smooth. Sprinkle 2 tablespoons walnuts over top and add dollops of cranberry sauce. Spread remaining batter over top and sprinkle with remaining 2 tablespoons nuts. Bake 18–22 minutes or until a toothpick inserted into center of cake comes out clean. Cool 1 hour before serving.

What Is Coffee Cake?

Coffee cake is designed to be enjoyed with coffee—hence the name. It is usually a slightly dense cake flavored with fruit, nuts, and spices. It is less sweet than other types of cake and often has sour cream or buttermilk added for a little tanginess. Coffee cakes can be unadorned or topped with a streusel or crumble topping. Thrifty home bakers of the past made coffee cakes to use up leftover fruits, nuts, and jams, so they were reducing waste and adding flavor!

COOKIE BUTTER CHEESECAKE

PREP TIME: 2¼ HOURS | COOK TIME: 30 MIN | SERVES 1

Cookie butter, a spread made from ground Belgian spice cookies called *speculoos*, has a devoted following. The creamy spread can be found in a variety of textures from creamy to crunchy and should be available in your grocery store where nut butters are sold.

INGREDIENTS

¼ cup plus 2 tablespoons *speculoos* cookie crumbs, divided

1 tablespoon granulated sugar

1 tablespoon unsalted butter, melted and cooled

2 ounces cream cheese, at room temperature

2 tablespoons creamy cookie butter

1 tablespoon packed light brown sugar

¼ teaspoon cornstarch

1 large egg yolk

1 tablespoon sour cream

1 teaspoon heavy cream

½ teaspoon pure vanilla extract

1. Preheat oven to 350°F and spray the bottom of a 4" springform pan with nonstick cooking spray.

2. In a small bowl, combine ¼ cup cookie crumbs, sugar, and butter. Mix until all crumbs are well coated in butter, then transfer crumb mixture to prepared pan and press to form a crust. Bake 8–10 minutes or until crust is firm, then remove from oven.

3. While crust is cooling, prepare filling. In a medium bowl, add cream cheese, cookie butter, and brown sugar. Use a hand mixer to beat on medium speed until smooth and creamy, about 2 minutes. Add cornstarch, egg yolk, and sour cream. Beat on medium speed until well combined, about 30 seconds. Add heavy cream and vanilla and mix on low speed until well incorporated, about 15 seconds.

4. Spread filling onto crust, then gently rap pan on counter three times to level mixture. Bake 22–25 minutes or until cheesecake is set around edges but still slightly jiggly in center. Cool in pan to room temperature, then transfer to an airtight container and refrigerate 2 hours. Garnish with remaining 2 tablespoons cookie crumbs before serving.

BLACK FOREST CAKE

PREP TIME: 10 MIN | COOK TIME: 23 MIN | YIELDS 1 (4") ROUND LAYER CAKE

If you have a can of cherry pie filling on hand, you can use ½ cup of it in this recipe in place of the cooked cherry filling.

INGREDIENTS

⅔ cup all-purpose flour

¼ cup Dutch-processed cocoa powder

½ teaspoon baking powder

¼ teaspoon salt

¼ cup salted butter, melted and cooled

½ cup granulated sugar

1 large egg yolk

2 tablespoons whole milk

¾ teaspoon pure vanilla extract, divided

½ cup boiling water

½ cup frozen dark sweet cherries, thawed, juices reserved

½ teaspoon cornstarch

½ cup heavy whipping cream

1 tablespoon powdered sugar

1 tablespoon kirsch liqueur, divided

1 tablespoon roughly grated dark chocolate

1. Preheat oven to 350°F and spray two 4" × 2" round cake pans with nonstick cooking spray.

2. In a medium bowl, sift together flour, cocoa powder, baking powder, and salt. Set aside.

3. In a small bowl, whisk together butter, granulated sugar, egg yolk, milk, and ½ teaspoon vanilla. Pour into flour mixture and stir until combined. Add boiling water in four additions, stirring after each addition.

4. Divide batter between prepared cake pans. Bake 18–22 minutes or until cakes spring back in center when gently pressed and edges come away from sides. Cool in pans 10 minutes before turning out onto wire racks to cool to room temperature.

5. In a small saucepan, add cherries with their juices and cornstarch. Heat over medium-low heat until cherry mixture is thick, about 5 minutes. Turn off heat and cool to room temperature.

6. In a medium bowl, add whipping cream, powdered sugar, and remaining ¼ teaspoon vanilla. Use a hand mixer to beat on low speed, about 10 seconds, then increase speed to medium and beat until cream forms soft peaks, about 1 minute.

7. To assemble, place one cake layer top-side down on a large plate. Brush cake with ½ tablespoon kirsch. Spread half of whipped cream on cake, top with cherries, then place second cake layer on top and brush with remaining kirsch. Spread remaining cream on top and garnish with chocolate. Serve immediately or refrigerate until ready.

CHAPTER 4

BREADS, ROLLS, AND BISCUITS

The smell of freshly baked bread makes the mouth water and evokes a feeling of comfort. Humans have been baking bread, in one form or another, for over thirty thousand years; bread is one of the earliest ways humans consumed grains. Rich in complex carbohydrates, bread is a significant form of energy and nutrition. It can be sliced and used for sandwiches, made into rolls, or rolled flat for wraps and tortillas. It is as versatile as it is delicious!

This chapter is all about the world of small-batch bread making. From crusty dinner rolls to flaky biscuits and petite loaves, this chapter offers you recipes for fresh bread without the worry of it going stale before you can enjoy it. From sweet breads like Small-Batch Cinnamon Rolls and Sticky Buns to savory staples like Cheesy Garlic Pull-Apart Bread and Ham and Cheddar Scones, and even more unusual breads like savory meat-stuffed Bierrocks with Beer Cheese Sauce and Korean Egg Bread (Gyeran Bbang), you can enjoy freshly baked breads for breakfast, lunch, and dinner in portions that are perfect for one.

SMALL-BATCH DINNER ROLLS

PREP TIME: 2 HOURS | COOK TIME: 19 MIN | YIELDS 4 ROLLS

These dinner rolls are soft, lightly sweet, and perfect as an addition to any meal. If you do not have bread flour, you can use only all-purpose flour.

INGREDIENTS

¼ cup whole milk

1 tablespoon granulated sugar

½ teaspoon dry active yeast

1 large egg yolk

2 tablespoons unsalted butter, melted and cooled

¼ teaspoon salt

½ cup all-purpose flour

½ cup bread flour

1. In a small microwave-safe bowl, heat milk on high for 20 seconds or until it reaches 110°F. Stir in sugar and yeast and allow to stand until yeast is bubbling and foamy, about 10 minutes.

2. To the work bowl of a stand mixer fitted with a dough hook, or in a large bowl using a wooden spoon, add yeast mixture, egg yolk, and butter. Mix on medium speed until well combined, then add salt and both flours and mix on low speed 1 minute. Increase speed to medium and knead 4 minutes or until dough is smooth. If mixing by hand, use the spoon to stir in the flour until it forms a shaggy ball, then knead in the bowl by hand until dough is smooth, about 10 minutes.

3. Form dough into a smooth ball, then cover bowl with a damp towel and let rise in a draft-free spot 1 hour or until doubled in bulk.

4. Preheat oven to 375°F and line a ¼ sheet pan or 8" × 8" cake pan with parchment.

5. Turn dough out onto a lightly floured surface. Press out any air bubbles with your palm. Divide the dough into four pieces and roll each into a smooth ball. Place dough balls on prepared pan. Cover with a damp towel and allow to rise 30 minutes.

6. Bake 18–20 minutes or until rolls are golden brown on top and bottom. Cool in pan 10 minutes before serving.

WHOLE-WHEAT CLOVERLEAF ROLLS

PREP TIME: 2 HOURS | COOK TIME: 19 MIN | YIELDS 4 ROLLS

If you do not want to make these into a cloverleaf shape you can divide the dough into four balls and make four regular rolls. Bake them in a 6" round cake pan so you can pull them apart and enjoy the soft edges!

INGREDIENTS

¼ cup whole milk

1 tablespoon honey

½ teaspoon dry active yeast

1 large egg yolk

2 tablespoons unsalted butter, melted and cooled

¼ teaspoon salt

¾ cup all-purpose flour

¼ cup whole-wheat flour

1. In a small microwave-safe bowl, heat milk on high for 20 seconds or until it reaches 110°F. Stir in honey and yeast and allow to stand until yeast is bubbling and foamy, about 10 minutes.

2. To the work bowl of a stand mixer fitted with a dough hook, or in a large bowl using a wooden spoon, add yeast mixture, egg yolk, and butter. Mix on medium speed until well combined, about 1 minute, then add salt and both flours and mix on low speed for 1 minute. Increase speed to medium and knead 4 minutes or until dough is smooth. If mixing by hand, use the spoon to stir in the flour until it forms a shaggy ball, then knead in the bowl by hand until dough is smooth, about 10 minutes.

3. Form dough into a smooth ball, then cover bowl with a damp towel and let rise in a draft-free spot 1 hour or until doubled in bulk.

4. Preheat oven to 375°F and spray four cups of a muffin pan with nonstick cooking spray.

5. Turn dough out onto a lightly floured surface. Press out any air bubbles with your palm. Divide the dough into twelve pieces and roll each into a smooth ball. Place three dough balls in each prepared cup. Cover with a damp towel and allow to rise 30 minutes or until rolls are puffy and a finger pressed into the side leaves a mark.

6. Bake 18–20 minutes or until rolls are golden brown on top and firm to the touch. Cool in pan 10 minutes before serving.

SMALL-BATCH SOFT PRETZELS

PREP TIME: 2 HOURS | COOK TIME: 14 MIN | YIELDS 2 PRETZELS

A quick dip into simmering baking soda water is what gives these pretzels their distinctive flavor and color. These are wonderful with the Beer Cheese Sauce from the Bierrocks recipe in this chapter. If you want, you can make these sweet by omitting the salt and brushing the hot pretzels with butter, then dusting them with cinnamon sugar.

INGREDIENTS

⅓ cup whole milk

1 tablespoon granulated sugar

½ teaspoon dry active yeast

1 large egg yolk

3 tablespoons unsalted butter, melted and cooled, divided

¼ teaspoon salt

1 cup all-purpose flour

6 cups water

⅓ cup baking soda

1 teaspoon coarse salt

1. In a small microwave-safe bowl, heat milk 20 seconds or until it reaches 110°F. Stir in sugar and yeast and allow to stand until yeast is bubbling and foamy, about 10 minutes.

2. To the work bowl of a stand mixer fitted with a dough hook, or a large bowl using a wooden spoon, add yeast mixture, egg yolk, and 2 tablespoons butter. Mix on medium speed until well combined, about 1 minute, then add salt and flour and mix on low speed for 1 minute. Increase speed to medium and knead 4 minutes or until dough is smooth. If mixing by hand, use the spoon to stir in the flour until it forms a shaggy ball, then knead in the bowl by hand until dough is smooth, about 10 minutes.

3. Form dough into a smooth ball, then cover bowl with a damp towel and let rise in a draft-free spot 1 hour or until doubled in bulk.

4. Preheat oven to 450°F and line a ¼ sheet pan with parchment. Spray parchment with nonstick cooking spray.

5. In a medium pot, add water and baking soda. Bring to a boil over high heat, about 10 minutes.

Continued on next page ▶

6 Turn dough out onto a lightly floured surface. Press out any air bubbles with your palm. Divide the dough into two pieces and roll each into a 25" rope. Form rope into a U shape, twist the two ends of the rope in the center, then press the ends down onto the bottom of the U to form a pretzel shape.

7 Carefully lower formed pretzels one at a time into boiling water and baking soda. Boil 40 seconds, then transfer to prepared baking pan. Sprinkle pretzels with coarse salt.

8 Bake 12–15 minutes or until pretzels are deeply golden brown on top and bottom. Brush with remaining 1 tablespoon butter and serve hot.

Pretzel Dogs

If you want to make these pretzels a complete meal you can transform them into pretzel dogs! Divide the dough into four pieces, roll each piece into a 10" rope, then wrap each rope around a hot dog that has been patted dry with a towel so the dough will stick. Be sure to pinch the end of the dough to the dough wrapped around the dog to prevent unraveling. Proceed with the recipe as directed and enjoy with yellow mustard!

SMALL-BATCH FRENCH BREAD

PREP TIME: 3 HOURS | COOK TIME: 21 MIN | YIELDS 1 (10") LOAF

Because French bread contains no fat, it does not keep well and is best eaten the day it is baked. If you have any left over, you can cube it, toss in a little olive oil, and bake in a 350°F oven for 10–12 minutes to make some spectacular croutons.

INGREDIENTS

⅓ cup water

¼ teaspoon granulated sugar

½ teaspoon dry active yeast

¼ teaspoon salt

¾ cup bread flour

1. In a small microwave-safe bowl, heat water on high for 20 seconds or until it reaches 110°F. Stir in sugar and yeast and allow to stand until yeast is bubbling and foamy, about 10 minutes.

2. To the work bowl of a stand mixer fitted with a dough hook, or in a large bowl using a wooden spoon, add yeast mixture, salt, and flour. Mix on low speed for 1 minute, then increase speed to medium and knead for 4 minutes or until dough is smooth. If mixing by hand, use the spoon to stir in the flour until it forms a shaggy ball, then knead in the bowl by hand until dough is smooth, about 10 minutes.

3. Form dough into a smooth ball, then cover bowl with a damp towel and let rise in a draft-free spot 1½ hours or until doubled in bulk.

4. Preheat oven to 425°F and line a ¼ sheet pan with parchment.

5. Turn dough out onto a lightly floured surface. Press out any air bubbles with your palm. Stretch dough into a 10"-long rectangle, then roll into a loaf shape. Tuck ends under, then roll gently to even loaf. Cover with a damp towel and let rise 1 hour.

6. With a sharp knife or razor blade, make three diagonal slashes down the loaf. Put loaf on prepared sheet pan and bake 20–25 minutes or until bread is deeply golden and sounds hollow when gently thumped on the side. Turn off oven, crack door 1", and let loaf cool fully in oven. Enjoy the same day as it is baked.

SMALL-BATCH HAMBURGER BUNS

PREP TIME: 2 HOURS | **COOK TIME: 19 MIN** | **YIELDS 4 BUNS**

These buns are big and fluffy, and they toast beautifully. You can also use these for breakfast sandwiches with egg, cheese, and your favorite meat or meat alternative, or use them for grilled chicken or fried fish sandwiches!

INGREDIENTS

⅓ cup water

2 teaspoons granulated sugar

½ teaspoon dry active yeast

1 large egg, beaten, divided

1 tablespoon unsalted butter, melted and cooled

½ teaspoon salt

1 cup bread flour

½ cup all-purpose flour

1 tablespoon sesame seeds

1. In a small microwave-safe bowl, heat water on high for 20 seconds or until it reaches 110°F. Stir in sugar and yeast and allow to stand until yeast is bubbling and foamy, about 10 minutes.

2. To the work bowl of a stand mixer fitted with a dough hook, add yeast mixture, half beaten egg, and butter. Mix on medium speed until well combined, about 1 minute, then add salt and both flours and mix on low speed for 1 minute. Increase speed to medium and knead 4 minutes or until dough is smooth.

3. Form dough into a smooth ball, then cover bowl with a damp towel and let rise in a draft-free spot 1 hour or until doubled in bulk.

4. Preheat oven to 375°F and line a ¼ sheet pan or 8" × 8" cake pan with parchment.

5. Turn dough out onto a lightly floured surface. Press out any air bubbles with your palm. Divide the dough into four pieces and roll each into a smooth ball. Place dough balls on prepared pan. Cover with a damp towel and allow to rise 45 minutes.

6. Brush tops of rolls with remaining half egg, then sprinkle sesame seeds over top. Bake 18–22 minutes or until buns are deeply golden brown on top and bottom and are firm to the touch. Cool to room temperature on pan before slicing in half and serving.

BIERROCKS WITH BEER CHEESE SAUCE

PREP TIME: 2½ HOURS | COOK TIME: 32 MIN | YIELDS 4 BUNS AND ¾ CUP SAUCE

Bierrocks are a German stuffed bun typically filled with ground beef, sauerkraut, and onion. They are also known as *runza* or *krautburger*. This recipe combines them with a beer cheese dipping sauce to make them extra fun to eat!

INGREDIENTS

¼ pound ground beef

¼ medium yellow onion, peeled and finely diced

¼ cup finely chopped prepared sauerkraut

½ cup whole milk

2 teaspoons granulated sugar

½ teaspoon dry active yeast

1 large egg, beaten, divided

½ teaspoon salt

1½ cups plus 1 teaspoon all-purpose flour, divided

1 tablespoon unsalted butter

⅛ teaspoon smoked paprika

½ cup lager beer

2 tablespoons heavy cream

¼ cup shredded sharp Cheddar cheese

1. In a medium nonstick skillet over medium heat, combine ground beef and onion. Cook until beef is browned and onion is soft, about 10 minutes. Remove from heat and drain excess grease. Stir in sauerkraut and set aside to cool.

2. In a small microwave-safe bowl, heat milk on high for 20 seconds or until it reaches 110°F. Stir in sugar and yeast and allow to stand until yeast is bubbling and foamy, about 10 minutes.

3. To the work bowl of a stand mixer fitted with a dough hook, or in a large bowl using a wooden spoon, add yeast mixture, half beaten egg, salt, and 1 cup flour. Mix on low speed for 1 minute, then increase speed to medium and knead for 4 minutes or until dough is smooth. If mixing by hand, use the spoon to stir in the flour until it forms a shaggy ball, then knead in the bowl by hand until dough is smooth, about 10 minutes.

4. Form dough into a smooth ball, then cover bowl with a damp towel and let rise in a draft-free spot 1 hour or until doubled in bulk.

5. Preheat oven to 375°F and line a ¼ sheet pan with parchment.

6. Turn dough out onto a lightly floured surface. Press out any air bubbles with your palm. Divide the dough into four pieces and flatten into a rough circle. Divide filling into the center of each piece of dough. Pull edges toward the center and pinch to seal. Place dough balls seam-side down on prepared pan. Cover with a damp towel and allow to rise 45 minutes or until buns are puffy and a finger pressed into the side leaves a mark.

7. Brush tops of rolls with remaining half egg. Bake 18–22 minutes or until buns are deeply golden brown on top and bottom and are firm to the touch. Cool 10 minutes before serving.

8. While buns bake, prepare cheese sauce. In a medium saucepan over medium-low heat, add butter. Once melted and foaming add remaining ½ cup plus 1 teaspoon flour and smoked paprika. Cook 1 minute or until flour is just golden brown. Slowly whisk in beer, making sure to whisk out any lumps, and cook until sauce starts to thicken, about 2 minutes. Add cream and whisk to combine, then remove from heat and whisk in cheese. If sauce is too thick add more cream to thin it out. Serve buns with cheese sauce for dipping.

CHEESY GARLIC PULL-APART BREAD

PREP TIME: 2 HOURS | COOK TIME: 16 MIN | YIELDS 8 ROLLS

These cheese-stuffed garlic rolls are a delicious snack while watching the big game, while enjoying Italian food, or anytime you need some cheese-stuffed comfort food. Serve these with a warm marinara sauce for dipping!

INGREDIENTS

¼ cup whole milk

1 teaspoon granulated sugar

½ teaspoon dry active yeast

1 large egg yolk

4 tablespoons unsalted butter, melted and cooled, divided

¼ teaspoon salt

½ cup all-purpose flour

½ cup bread flour

¼ teaspoon garlic powder

2 sticks mozzarella string cheese, each cut into four pieces

1 medium clove garlic, peeled and minced

1. In a small microwave-safe bowl, heat milk on high for 20 seconds or until it reaches 110°F. Stir in sugar and yeast and allow to stand until yeast is bubbling and foamy, about 10 minutes.

2. To the work bowl of a stand mixer fitted with a dough hook, or in a large bowl using a wooden spoon, add yeast mixture, egg yolk, and 2 table-spoons butter. Mix on medium speed until well combined, about 1 minute, then add salt, both flours, and garlic powder and mix on low speed for 1 minute. Increase speed to medium and knead 4 minutes or until dough is smooth. If mixing by hand, use the spoon to stir in the flour until it forms a shaggy ball, then knead in the bowl by hand until dough is smooth, about 10 minutes.

3. Form dough into a smooth ball, then cover bowl with a damp towel and let rise in a draft-free spot 1 hour or until doubled in bulk.

4. Preheat oven to 375°F and spray a 6" round cake pan with nonstick cooking spray.

5. Turn dough out onto a lightly floured surface. Press out any air bubbles with your palm. Divide the dough into eight pieces. Flatten each piece into a rough circle, place a piece of mozzarella

in the center, then tuck the edges over cheese. Roll each piece of dough-wrapped cheese into a smooth ball and place in prepared pan. Cover with a damp towel and allow to rise 30 minutes or until rolls are puffy and a finger pressed into the side leaves a mark.

6 While rolls rise, prepare garlic butter. In a small microwave-safe bowl, add remaining 2 tablespoons butter and garlic. Microwave 30 seconds or until butter is sizzling and garlic is fragrant. Set aside.

7 Bake rolls 14–16 minutes or until they are golden brown on top and feel firm to the touch. While still hot, brush with garlic butter. Cool 10 minutes before serving.

Pizza and Nacho Rolls

If you want to make these into a pizza-flavored treat add your favorite pizza toppings into each dough ball before shaping. Some ideas include a slice or two of pepperoni, some crumbled cooked Italian sausage, finely chopped onions and peppers, sliced olives, or chopped ham and pineapple. If you are adding raw vegetables, be sure to chop them very finely so they will be cooked through. For a more Tex-Mex flair, swap the mozzarella for cubed Cheddar and add a slice of pickled jalapeño for a spicy kick, and dip it in salsa!

STICKY BUNS

PREP TIME: 2 HOURS | COOK TIME: 23 MIN | YIELDS 4 ROLLS

Feel free to swap the nuts in the topping to any you have on hand that you like. Walnuts or even peanuts would be a fun twist. You can also add up to ¼ cup of raisins, dried cranberries, or chopped dried cherries to the cinnamon filling for bursts of fruity flavor.

INGREDIENTS

¼ cup whole milk

2 tablespoons granulated sugar

½ teaspoon dry active yeast

1 large egg yolk

7 tablespoons unsalted butter, melted and cooled, divided

¼ teaspoon salt

½ cup all-purpose flour

½ cup bread flour

2 teaspoons dry milk powder

½ cup packed light brown sugar, divided

1 teaspoon ground cinnamon

1 tablespoon honey

⅔ cup chopped pecans

1. In a small microwave-safe bowl, heat milk 20 seconds or until it reaches 110°F. Stir in granulated sugar and yeast and allow to stand until yeast is bubbling and foamy, about 10 minutes.

2. To the work bowl of a stand mixer fitted with a dough hook, or in a large bowl using a wooden spoon, add yeast mixture, egg yolk, and 3 tablespoons butter. Mix on medium speed until well combined, about 1 minute, then add salt, both flours, and milk powder. Mix on low speed for 1 minute, then increase speed to medium and knead 4 minutes or until dough is smooth. If mixing by hand, use the spoon to stir in the flour until it forms a shaggy ball, then knead in the bowl by hand until dough is smooth, about 10 minutes.

3. Form dough into a smooth ball, then cover bowl with a damp towel and let rise in a draft-free spot 1 hour or until doubled in bulk.

4. In a small bowl, combine 1 tablespoon butter, ¼ cup brown sugar, and cinnamon. Mix until well combined. Set aside.

5. In a small saucepan, add remaining ¼ cup brown sugar, remaining 3 tablespoons butter, honey, and pecans. Heat over medium heat until brown sugar is melted and starting to simmer around the edges, about 4 minutes.

6. Preheat oven to 375°F and spray a 6" round cake pan with nonstick cooking spray. Pour pecan mixture into prepared pan and spread to edges. Set aside.

7. Turn dough out onto a lightly floured surface. Press out any air bubbles with your palm. Roll dough out into a ½"-thick rectangle approximately 4" × 6". Spread cinnamon mixture over dough, then roll dough along the long edge into a spiral. Slice into four rolls and place in prepared pan on top of pecan mixture. Cover with a damp towel and allow to rise 30 minutes or until rolls are puffy and a finger pressed into the side leaves a mark.

8. Bake 18–20 minutes or until rolls are golden brown on top and feel firm to the touch. Immediately, but carefully, turn buns onto a serving plate. Cool 15 minutes before serving.

GARLIC KNOTS

PREP TIME: 2 HOURS | COOK TIME: 25 MIN | YIELDS 4 ROLLS

These Garlic Knots are the perfect accompaniment to Italian food, steak dinners, or a hearty bowl of soup. If you prefer not to buy a whole bulb of garlic for this recipe, you can find chunky garlic paste in most produce departments. It keeps for weeks in the refrigerator and tastes better than ready-chopped garlic from a jar.

INGREDIENTS

¼ cup whole milk

1 teaspoon granulated sugar

½ teaspoon dry active yeast

1 large egg yolk

4 tablespoons unsalted butter, melted and cooled, divided

¼ teaspoon salt

½ cup all-purpose flour

½ cup bread flour

2 medium cloves garlic, chopped (about 1 tablespoon)

1 teaspoon dried basil

1 tablespoon freshly grated Parmesan cheese

1. In a small microwave-safe bowl, heat milk on high for 20 seconds or until it reaches 110°F. Stir in sugar and yeast and allow to stand until yeast is bubbling and foamy, about 10 minutes.

2. To the work bowl of a stand mixer fitted with a dough hook, or in a large bowl using a wooden spoon, add yeast mixture, egg yolk, and 2 table-spoons butter. Mix on medium speed until well combined, about 1 minute, then add salt and both flours and mix on low speed for 1 minute. Increase speed to medium and knead 4 minutes or until dough is smooth. If mixing by hand, use the spoon to stir in the flour until it forms a shaggy ball, then knead in the bowl by hand until dough is smooth, about 10 minutes.

3. Form dough into a smooth ball, then cover bowl with a damp towel and let rise in a draft-free spot 1 hour or until doubled in bulk.

4. Preheat oven to 375°F and line a ¼ sheet pan or 8" × 8" cake pan with parchment.

5. Turn dough out onto a lightly floured surface. Press out any air bubbles with your palm. Divide the dough into four pieces and roll each into a 6"-long rope. Tie each rope into a simple knot, then place on prepared pan. Cover with a damp towel and allow to rise 30 minutes or until rolls are puffy and a finger pressed into the side leaves a mark.

6. While knots rise, prepare garlic butter topping. In a small saucepan, add remaining 2 tablespoons butter and garlic. Heat over low heat until garlic is fragrant, about 5 minutes. Turn off heat and stir in basil. Set aside.

7. Bake rolls 18–20 minutes or until they are golden brown on top and bottom. Take knots out of oven and brush with garlic butter. Sprinkle each knot with Parmesan. Serve hot.

SMALL-BATCH CINNAMON ROLLS

PREP TIME: 2 HOURS | COOK TIME: 19 MIN | YIELDS 4 ROLLS

You can prepare these rolls the night before serving, cover them with plastic wrap or reusable beeswax paper, and place them in the refrigerator overnight to rise. Pull them out to stand at room temperature 1 hour before you plan to bake them so the yeast has a chance to wake up.

INGREDIENTS

¼ cup whole milk

2 tablespoons granulated sugar

½ teaspoon dry active yeast

1 large egg yolk

5 tablespoons unsalted butter, melted and cooled, divided

¼ teaspoon salt

½ cup all-purpose flour

½ cup bread flour

2 teaspoons dry milk powder

¼ cup packed light brown sugar

1 teaspoon ground cinnamon

1. In a small microwave-safe bowl, heat milk 20 seconds or until it reaches 110°F. Stir in granulated sugar and yeast and allow to stand until yeast is bubbling and foamy, about 10 minutes.

2. To the work bowl of a stand mixer fitted with a dough hook, or a large bowl using a wooden spoon, add yeast mixture, egg yolk, and 2 tablespoons butter. Mix on medium speed until well combined, then add salt, both flours, and milk powder. Mix on low speed 1 minute, then increase speed to medium and knead 4 minutes or until dough is smooth. If mixing by hand, use the spoon to stir in the flour until it forms a shaggy ball, then knead in the bowl by hand until dough is smooth, about 10 minutes.

3. Form dough into a smooth ball, then cover bowl with a damp towel and let rise in a draft-free spot 1 hour or until doubled in bulk.

4. In a small bowl, combine remaining 3 tablespoons butter, brown sugar, and cinnamon. Mix until well combined. Set aside.

5. Preheat oven to 375°F and spray an 8" round cake pan with nonstick cooking spray.

Continued on next page ▶

6 Turn dough out onto a lightly floured surface. Press out any air bubbles with your palm. Roll dough out into a ½"-thick rectangle approximately 10" × 12". Spread cinnamon mixture over dough, then roll dough along the long edge into a log. Slice into four rolls and place 1" apart in prepared pan. Cover with a damp towel and allow to rise 30 minutes or until rolls are puffy and a finger pressed into the side leaves a mark.

7 Bake 18–20 minutes or until rolls are golden brown on top and bottom. Cool in pan 5 minutes before serving.

Cinnamon Roll Frosting

If you like creamy frosting on your cinnamon rolls you should try this recipe. Mix 1 tablespoon melted butter, 2 teaspoons milk, and ¼ teaspoon vanilla with ¾ cup powdered sugar. Whisk until it forms a smooth glaze that is thick but pourable, like pancake batter. If you like your glaze a little thinner, add a little extra milk ½ teaspoon at a time. This spreads best over warm, not hot, cinnamon rolls, and the frosting will melt a little into the rolls, adding more sweetness in each bite, so let the cinnamon rolls cool at least 15 minutes before frosting.

SMALL-BATCH FLOUR TORTILLAS

PREP TIME: 10 MIN | COOK TIME: 5 MIN | YIELDS 4 TORTILLAS

Nothing beats the flavor of a freshly griddled flour tortilla. These tortillas make excellent breakfast tacos, soft tacos, quesadillas, or sandwich wraps. If you have lard, use that instead of shortening to give these tortillas a more authentic flavor.

INGREDIENTS

½ cup all-purpose flour

⅛ teaspoon salt

⅛ teaspoon baking powder

1 tablespoon vegetable shortening

¼ cup warm milk

1. In a medium bowl, add flour, salt, and baking powder. Whisk to combine.

2. Add shortening and use your fingers to rub it into the flour until flour resembles coarse sand. Stir in milk and knead until dough forms a smooth ball, 8–10 minutes.

3. Turn dough out onto a lightly floured surface and divide into four balls. Cover dough balls with a damp cloth and let rest 30 minutes.

4. Once rested, roll dough balls into 6" circles. Cover with a damp towel.

5. While dough is resting, place a griddle or cast iron skillet over medium heat. Once hot, add one to two tortillas, depending on the size of the griddle. Cook until tortillas start to puff and the bottoms have dark brown spots, 1–2 minutes. Flip and cook until the second side is golden brown and the tortillas are steaming hot, 1–2 minutes more. Transfer to a large plate and cover with a dry towel while you repeat with remaining dough. Serve warm.

CHINESE-STYLE STEAMED BUNS

Char siu sauce is a Chinese-style barbecue sauce found in most grocery stores in the Asian food section. It is a sweet, sticky sauce flavored with white pepper, five-spice, and hoisin sauce. If you can't find it, you can use 2 tablespoons of hoisin sauce with ¼ teaspoon five-spice powder.

INGREDIENTS

3 teaspoons vegetable oil, divided

⅓ pound ground pork

1 teaspoon minced garlic

1 medium green onion, green part only, chopped

2 tablespoons char siu sauce

5 tablespoons water, heated to 100°F, divided

¼ cup plus 3 tablespoons all-purpose flour

1 teaspoon active dry yeast

2 teaspoons granulated sugar, divided

¼ cup cake flour

½ teaspoon baking powder

¼ teaspoon salt

1. In a medium skillet over medium heat, add 2 teaspoons oil. Once hot, add pork, garlic, and onion and cook until pork is cooked through, about 10 minutes. Add char siu sauce and stir to combine. Cook until pork mixture is thick and sticky, about 5 minutes. Turn off heat and cool to room temperature before refrigerating until ready to use.

2. In a medium bowl, combine 3 tablespoons hot water, 3 tablespoons all-purpose flour, yeast, and 1 teaspoon sugar. Mix until smooth, cover with a damp towel, and let stand at room temperature 1 hour or until very bubbly.

3. To mixture, add remaining 1 teaspoon oil, remaining 2 tablespoons hot water, remaining ¼ cup all-purpose flour, remaining 1 teaspoon sugar, cake flour, baking powder, and salt and mix until a smooth ball of dough forms. Cover bowl with a damp towel and let rise 4 hours.

4. Turn dough out onto a lightly floured surface and use your palm to gently press out air bubbles. Divide dough into four pieces and shape each into a circle that is thick in the center and thinner around the edges. Divide pork mixture between

dough pieces, then wrap dough around filling and pinch to close. Place dough pinched-side down and use a cupped palm to roll with a circular motion to shape into a smooth ball.

5. Place buns on small squares of parchment, cover with a damp towel, and let rise 1 hour.

6. While buns rise, prepare steamer. Place a steamer basket and lid over a pot filled with water and bring to a boil.

7. Carefully place buns with their parchment into prepared steamer. Cover and let steam 10 minutes or until buns are puffed, shiny, and firm to the touch. Serve hot.

Optional Steamed Bun Fillings

Steamed buns can be filled with any number of delicious things and can be used as a main dish, side dish, or snack. Some different filling options include prepared sweet red bean paste, stir-fried cabbage with minced chicken and hoisin sauce, chopped shrimp, stir-fried green onion with garlic, or roasted and mashed Korean yam. You can also leave them unfilled and serve with roasted pork, duck, or your favorite stir-fry.

EASY SKILLET FLATBREAD

PREP TIME: 10 MIN | COOK TIME: 2 MIN | YIELDS 2 FLATBREADS

These flatbreads work best with full-fat Greek yogurt, but if you do not have any, you can use low-fat yogurt and stir in 1 teaspoon of olive oil. If you have self-rising flour, you can use ½ cup of that in place of the dry ingredients.

INGREDIENTS

½ cup all-purpose flour

½ teaspoon baking powder

¼ teaspoon baking soda

¼ teaspoon salt

½ cup full-fat plain Greek yogurt

1. In a medium bowl, add flour, baking powder, baking soda, and salt. Whisk to combine.

2. Add yogurt and mix until mixture just forms a ball.

3. Turn dough out onto a lightly floured surface and divide into two balls. Cover dough balls with a damp cloth and let rest 10 minutes.

4. Once rested, roll dough balls into 8" circles.

5. Place a griddle or cast iron skillet over medium heat. Once hot, add one to two flatbreads, depending on the size of the griddle, and cook until puffed and browned, 1–2 minutes. Flip and cook until the second side is golden brown and the flatbread is steaming hot, 1–2 minutes more. Transfer to a large plate and cover with a dry towel while you repeat with remaining dough. Serve warm.

DOUGHNUT HOLES

PREP TIME: 10 MIN | COOK TIME: 4 MIN | YIELDS 6 DOUGHNUT HOLES

Fresh, homemade doughnuts are a wonderful treat, and this recipe makes just the right amount for one person to enjoy! If you like, you can swap the whole milk for buttermilk for a tangier doughnut. If you do, also add a pinch of nutmeg to add even more flavor!

INGREDIENTS

Oil, for frying

½ cup powdered sugar

¼ teaspoon ground cinnamon

½ cup all-purpose flour

1 tablespoon granulated sugar

¼ teaspoon baking powder

⅛ teaspoon salt

1 large egg yolk

¼ cup whole milk

1 teaspoon unsalted butter, melted

¼ teaspoon pure vanilla extract

1. In a large heavy-bottom pot with deep sides, add 2" oil over medium-high heat until it reaches 350°F.

2. In a medium bowl, add powdered sugar and cinnamon. Stir to combine then set aside.

3. In a separate medium bowl, add flour, granulated sugar, baking powder, and salt. Whisk to combine.

4. In a small bowl, whisk together egg yolk, milk, butter, and vanilla. Pour wet ingredients into dry and mix until batter is smooth.

5. Using a cookie scoop or two spoons, carefully drop 1" balls of batter into heated oil. Fry 2 minutes per side or until golden brown all over. Remove from oil and drain on a paper towel–lined plate 1 minute, then toss in powdered sugar mixture. Enjoy warm.

Filled Doughnut Holes

If you like, you can add filling to your doughnut holes. You will need a piping bag or heavy-duty freezer bag and a round metal piping tip. Snip the tip off the end of the bag, or one corner of a freezer bag, and add the metal tip. All you need to do now is load the filling of your choice into the bag, press the tip into the doughnut hole, and squeeze the filling until it just starts to come out from around the piping tip. Seedless strawberry or raspberry jam is a popular choice, but you could also fill your doughnuts with prepared chocolate or vanilla pudding, prepared lemon curd, or dulce de leche!

BAKED CINNAMON SUGAR DOUGHNUTS

PREP TIME: 10 MIN | COOK TIME: 9 MIN | YIELDS 2 DOUGHNUTS

Baked doughnuts are best the day they are made, so most recipes will make far too many for one person to enjoy before they go stale. This recipe solves that problem by making two fluffy, cinnamon sugar–coated doughnuts perfect for one person to enjoy!

INGREDIENTS

¼ cup all-purpose flour

¼ teaspoon baking powder

⅛ teaspoon baking soda

⅛ teaspoon salt

1 large egg yolk

1 tablespoon plus 2 teaspoons packed light brown sugar

2 tablespoons sour cream

1 tablespoon plus 1½ teaspoons unsalted butter, melted, divided

¼ teaspoon pure vanilla extract

¼ cup granulated sugar

¼ teaspoon ground cinnamon

1. Preheat oven to 350°F and spray two cups of a doughnut pan with nonstick cooking spray.

2. In a medium bowl, combine flour, baking powder, baking soda, and salt. Whisk to combine and set aside.

3. In a small bowl, combine egg yolk, brown sugar, sour cream, 1½ teaspoons butter, and vanilla. Whisk to combine, then add to dry ingredients and mix until batter is smooth.

4. Divide batter between prepared doughnut cups, making sure to smooth batter on top. Bake 9–11 minutes or until edges are golden brown and doughnut springs back when gently pressed in the center. Cool in pan 2 minutes, then turn out onto a wire rack and let stand until cool enough to touch.

5. In a shallow bowl, combine granulated sugar and cinnamon and mix well. Brush warm doughnuts with remaining 1 tablespoon butter, then dredge doughnuts in cinnamon sugar. Enjoy warm.

FLAKY BISCUITS

PREP TIME: 30 MIN | COOK TIME: 18 MIN | YIELDS 4 BISCUITS

Flaky biscuits are a thing of beauty. The trick to a perfectly flaky biscuit is to fold and press your dough instead of traditional kneading. Folding and pressing will give you the delicious layers you desire! If you do not have bread flour, you can swap it with all-purpose flour.

INGREDIENTS

¼ cup plus 1 teaspoon all-purpose flour

¼ cup plus 1 teaspoon bread flour

½ teaspoon baking powder

½ teaspoon granulated sugar

¼ teaspoon salt

3 tablespoons cubed salted butter, chilled

3 tablespoons cold buttermilk

1. Preheat oven to 350°F and line a baking sheet with parchment or a reusable silicone baking mat.

2. In a medium bowl, combine flours, baking powder, sugar, and salt. Whisk well to combine. Add butter and use your fingers to rub mixture until butter is in pea-sized pieces and flour resembles coarse sand. Cover and chill 10 minutes.

3. Make a well in dry ingredients and add buttermilk. Gently stir until it just forms a shaggy ball. Turn out onto a lightly floured surface and press dough into a ½"-thick rectangle, then fold dough in half. Turn the dough a quarter turn and repeat this process four more times. You may need to use a spatula or bench scraper the first few times, as dough will be shaggy. Cover dough and chill 10 minutes.

4. Once the dough is chilled, use your hands to form dough into a 5" × 3" rectangle approximately ½" thick. Use a sharp chef's knife to cut dough into four squares by pressing straight down and lifting straight up. This will help your layers to stay separate. Transfer biscuits to prepared baking sheet.

5. Bake 18–20 minutes or until biscuits are puffed and golden brown. Cool on the baking sheet 5 minutes before enjoying.

GARLIC CHEESE BISCUITS

PREP TIME: 10 MIN | COOK TIME: 14 MIN | YIELDS 4 BISCUITS

If you are a fan of the garlic cheese biscuits served by a popular seafood chain restaurant, you are going to love these! Packed with plenty of sharp cheddar and topped with an herb and garlic butter glaze, these biscuits are perfect with seafood, steaks, or chicken.

INGREDIENTS

½ cup plus 1 tablespoon all-purpose flour

¼ teaspoon baking powder

⅛ teaspoon baking soda

¼ teaspoon granulated sugar

⅛ teaspoon garlic powder

⅛ teaspoon onion powder

3 tablespoons cubed salted butter, chilled

3 tablespoons buttermilk

⅓ cup finely shredded sharp Cheddar cheese

2 tablespoons salted butter, at room temperature

1 teaspoon minced garlic

½ teaspoon dried chives

1. Preheat oven to 350°F and line a baking sheet with parchment or a reusable silicone baking mat.

2. In a medium bowl, combine flour, baking powder, baking soda, sugar, garlic powder, and onion powder. Whisk well to combine. Add cubed butter and use your fingers to rub mixture until it resembles coarse sand.

3. Make a well in dry ingredients and add buttermilk. Gently stir two times, then add cheese and stir until a shaggy batter forms and no dry flour remains.

4. Scoop batter onto prepared baking sheet in four equal mounds. Bake 12–15 minutes or until biscuits are puffed and golden brown.

5. While biscuits bake, add butter, garlic, and chives to a small saucepan. Heat over medium-low heat until butter is melted and garlic is fragrant, 2–3 minutes. Remove from heat and let cool.

6. Once biscuits come out of oven, brush with garlic butter mixture. Cool on the baking sheet 5 minutes before serving.

CINNAMON PULL-APART BREAD

PREP TIME: 20 MIN | COOK TIME: 15 MIN | SERVES 1

This personal-sized version of the classic monkey bread is made with biscuit dough rather than yeast dough, so it is easier and faster than the classic.

INGREDIENTS

⅓ cup all-purpose flour

1 tablespoon granulated sugar

¼ teaspoon baking powder

1½ tablespoons cubed salted butter, chilled

2 tablespoons cold buttermilk

2 tablespoons salted butter, melted

¼ teaspoon pure vanilla extract

2 tablespoons packed light brown sugar

¼ teaspoon ground cinnamon

1. Preheat oven to 350°F and spray an 8-ounce ramekin with nonstick cooking spray.

2. In a medium bowl, combine flour, granulated sugar, and baking powder. Whisk well to combine. Add cubed butter and use your fingers to rub mixture until butter is in pea-sized pieces and flour resembles coarse sand.

3. Make a well in dry ingredients and add buttermilk. Gently stir until it just forms a shaggy ball. Turn out onto a lightly floured surface and press dough into a ¼"-thick rectangle, then fold dough in half. Turn the dough a quarter turn and repeat this process four more times. You may need to use a spatula the first few times, as the dough will be shaggy. Cover dough and chill 10 minutes.

4. Once the dough is chilled, use a sharp chef's knife to cut dough into twelve small pieces by pressing straight down and lifting straight up. This will help your layers to stay separate.

5. In a small bowl, combine melted butter and vanilla. In a separate small bowl, combine brown sugar and cinnamon. Mix well.

6. Dip biscuit pieces into butter, then roll in cinnamon sugar. Place into ramekin. Top with any remaining butter and cinnamon sugar.

7. Bake 15–17 minutes or until biscuits are puffed and sides are bubbling. Cool 3 minutes, then run a knife around edge to loosen and turn out onto a medium plate. Enjoy warm.

IRISH SODA BREAD

PREP TIME: 10 MIN | COOK TIME: 20 MIN | YIELDS 1 LOAF

Soda bread is traditionally just flour, baking soda, salt, and buttermilk. This version adds a little sugar and an egg yolk for extra richness. The raisins are totally optional and can be left out or replaced with any dried fruit you enjoy. You can also swap them for chocolate chips for a sweeter version.

INGREDIENTS

½ cup all-purpose flour

1 tablespoon granulated sugar

¼ teaspoon baking powder

⅛ teaspoon baking soda

2 tablespoons cubed salted butter, chilled

¼ cup raisins

¼ cup buttermilk

1 large egg yolk

1. Preheat oven to 425°F and line a baking sheet with parchment or a reusable silicone baking mat.

2. In a medium bowl, combine flour, sugar, baking powder, and baking soda. Whisk to combine. Add cubed butter and use your fingers to rub mixture until butter is in pea-sized pieces and flour resembles coarse sand. Toss in raisins.

3. In a small bowl, whisk together buttermilk and egg yolk. Add to dry ingredients and mix until a shaggy dough forms. Turn dough out onto a lightly floured surface and gently knead three to five times or until dough is smooth.

4. Shape dough into a 4" ball and place on prepared baking sheet. Use a sharp knife to cut a cross pattern into top of dough about ½" deep.

5. Bake 20–25 minutes or until bread is golden brown and a toothpick or wooden skewer inserted into the center of loaf comes out clean. Cool on the baking sheet 10 minutes, then transfer to a rack to cool until just warm. Serve warm or at room temperature.

HAM AND CHEDDAR SCONES

PREP TIME: 30 MIN | COOK TIME: 15 MIN | YIELDS 4 SCONES

Scones are a bit denser and crumblier than biscuits, so they are perfect for slathering with soft butter, clotted cream, or whipped cream cheese! These savory scones are perfect for breakfast, served as a midday snack, or enjoyed with a warm bowl of soup or stew!

INGREDIENTS

⅔ cup all-purpose flour

½ teaspoon baking powder

½ teaspoon granulated sugar

⅛ teaspoon salt

2 tablespoons cubed salted butter, chilled

¼ cup shredded sharp Cheddar cheese

¼ cup chopped smoked ham

¼ cup cold heavy cream

1 large egg yolk

1. Preheat oven to 350°F and line a baking sheet with parchment or a reusable silicone baking mat.

2. In a medium bowl, combine flour, baking powder, sugar, and salt. Whisk well to combine. Add butter and use your fingers to rub mixture until butter is in pea-sized pieces and flour resembles coarse sand. Toss in cheese and ham and mix well. Cover and chill 10 minutes.

3. Make a well in dry ingredients and add cream and egg yolk. Gently whisk egg yolk with cream, then stir in flour until it just forms a shaggy ball. Turn out onto a lightly floured surface and press dough into a ½"-thick rectangle, then fold dough in half. Turn the dough a quarter turn and repeat this process four more times. You may need to use a spatula or bench scraper the first few times, as the dough will be shaggy. Cover dough and chill 10 minutes.

4. Once the dough is chilled, use your hands to form dough into a ¾"-thick circle. Use a sharp chef's knife to cut dough into four wedges by pressing straight down and lifting straight up. Transfer wedges to prepared baking sheet.

5. Bake 15–18 minutes or until scones are puffed and golden brown. Cool on the baking sheet 5 minutes before enjoying.

MINI-JAPANESE MILK BREAD

PREP TIME: 3 HOURS | COOK TIME: 25 MIN | YIELDS 6 (½") SLICES

This recipe super-hydrates a portion of the flour with milk so the bread ends up staying fresher longer. This loaf of soft and chewy bread is just the right size for one person to enjoy over a couple of days for making sandwiches, toasting, or to make Classic Bread Pudding (see Chapter 6).

INGREDIENTS

¼ cup heavy cream, divided

¼ cup water, divided

½ cup all-purpose flour, divided

½ cup bread flour, divided

1 teaspoon active dry yeast

1 tablespoon granulated sugar, divided

1 teaspoon dry milk powder

½ teaspoon salt

1 large egg white

1 tablespoon unsalted butter, melted and cooled

1. In a small saucepan, add 2 tablespoons cream, 2 tablespoons water, 2 tablespoons all-purpose flour, and 2 tablespoons bread flour. Whisk until smooth, then cook, stirring constantly, over medium heat until mixture becomes very thick and forms a ball around the spatula. Remove from heat and cool 20 minutes.

2. In a small microwave-safe bowl, heat remaining 2 tablespoons water on high in 20-second intervals until it reaches 100°F. Stir in yeast and 1 teaspoon sugar and mix well. Let stand 10 minutes or until foamy and bubbling.

3. Place cooked flour mixture into work bowl of a stand mixer fitted with the dough hook. Add remaining ingredients along with yeast mixture. Mix on low speed for 2 minutes, then increase speed to medium and mix 4 minutes or until dough forms a smooth ball around the hook. The dough should be a little sticky but not wet to the touch. If it clings to your fingers add more all-purpose flour a teaspoon at a time until the proper texture is reached.

4. Turn dough out onto a work surface dusted with flour. Gently knead dough, adding flour to keep it from sticking, 3 minutes, then form into a smooth ball and place in a lightly greased bowl. Cover with a damp towel and allow to rise until doubled in bulk, about 1½ hours.

5. Preheat oven to 350°F and spray an 8" loaf pan with nonstick cooking spray.

6. Once risen, turn dough out onto a lightly floured surface and use your palm to press dough flat. Once flat, use your fingertips to poke holes in dough to make sure it is thoroughly degassed. You do not want any large gas bubbles to remain.

7. Divide dough into two equal pieces. Form each piece into an 11"-long log. Twist the logs together to form a loaf and transfer to prepared loaf pan. Cover with a damp towel and allow to proof until dough is puffy and a finger pressed into dough leaves an imprint, about 45 minutes.

8. Bake 20–25 minutes or until bread is golden brown all over and sounds hollow when gently thumped on the side. Cool in pan 10 minutes before turning out onto a wire rack to cool to room temperature.

HONEY BUTTER BISCUITS

PREP TIME: 10 MIN | COOK TIME: 14 MIN | YIELDS 4 BISCUITS

These biscuits are light and fluffy and provide the perfect accompaniment to a savory dinner by adding a sweet touch to help cleanse the palate. Because they are drenched in honey butter as they come out of the oven there is no need to add any extra butter when serving—unless you want to!

INGREDIENTS

½ cup plus 1 tablespoon all-purpose flour

¼ teaspoon baking powder

⅛ teaspoon baking soda

⅛ teaspoon salt

3 tablespoons cubed salted butter, chilled, divided

3 tablespoons buttermilk

2 tablespoons honey, divided

1. Preheat oven to 350°F and line a baking sheet with parchment or a reusable silicone baking mat.

2. In a medium bowl, combine flour, baking powder, baking soda, and salt. Whisk well to combine. Add 2 tablespoons butter and use your fingers to rub mixture until it resembles coarse sand.

3. Make a well in dry ingredients and add buttermilk and 1 tablespoon honey. Gently stir until a shaggy batter forms and no dry flour remains.

4. Scoop batter onto prepared baking sheet in four equal mounds. Bake 12–15 minutes or until biscuits are puffed and golden brown.

5. While biscuits bake, prepare honey butter. In a small microwave-safe bowl, add remaining 1 tablespoon butter and remaining 1 tablespoon honey and heat in 20-second intervals, stirring well between each interval, until melted. Set aside.

6. When biscuits come out of oven brush them with honey butter. Cool on the baking sheet 5 minutes before enjoying.

KOREAN EGG BREAD (GYERAN BBANG)

PREP TIME: 10 MIN | COOK TIME: 20 MIN | YIELDS 2 BREADS

Korean egg bread is a popular street food in South Korea during the cooler months. It is essentially a sweet pancake that is grilled in an oval-shaped mold with a whole egg inside. Think of it as an all-in-one breakfast! Enjoy these warm for the best flavor.

INGREDIENTS

1 large egg white

2 tablespoons salted butter, melted

1 tablespoon granulated sugar

2 teaspoons whole milk

⅛ teaspoon pure vanilla extract

3 tablespoons all-purpose flour

¼ teaspoon baking powder

2 large eggs

1. Preheat oven to 350°F and spray two cups of a muffin pan with nonstick cooking spray.

2. In a small bowl, combine egg white, butter, sugar, milk, and vanilla. Mix well.

3. In a medium bowl, combine flour and baking powder. Whisk to combine, then pour egg mixture into dry ingredients and mix until a smooth batter forms.

4. Fill each prepared muffin cup ¼ full with batter. Crack 1 egg into each cup, then top with remaining batter. Make sure egg is mostly covered.

5. Bake 20–25 minutes or until muffins are golden brown and a toothpick inserted into the center comes out clean. Cool in pan 5 minutes before turning out onto a large plate. Serve warm.

PERSONAL PIZZA CRUST

PREP TIME: 1½ HOURS | COOK TIME: 9 MIN | YIELDS 1 CRUST

The beauty of a personal pizza is you can top it any way you want! From red sauce to pesto, and pepperoni to mushroom, the only limits are your imagination. If you are going to use a pizza stone, be sure to add it to the oven before heating so it warms evenly, making the crust even crisper on the outside and fluffy on the inside.

INGREDIENTS

¼ cup water

1 tablespoon granulated sugar

½ teaspoon dry active yeast

½ cup bread flour

⅛ teaspoon salt

¼ teaspoon olive oil

1. In a small microwave-safe bowl, heat water 20 seconds or until it reaches 110°F. Stir in sugar and yeast and allow to stand until yeast is bubbling and foamy, about 10 minutes.

2. To the work bowl of a stand mixer fitted with a dough hook, or in a large bowl using a wooden spoon, add yeast mixture with remaining ingredients. Mix on low speed until just combined, about 1 minute, then increase speed to medium and knead 4 minutes or until dough is smooth. If mixing by hand, use the spoon to stir in flour until it forms a shaggy ball, then knead in the bowl by hand until dough is smooth, about 10 minutes.

3. Form dough into a smooth ball, then cover bowl with a damp towel and let rise in a draft-free spot 1 hour or until doubled in bulk.

4. Preheat oven to 450°F.

5. Turn dough out onto a lightly floured surface. Press out any air bubbles with your palm. Stretch dough into a circle 8"–10" wide. Transfer dough to a baking sheet or pizza pan.

6. Bake 3–4 minutes or until crust is par-baked and starting to bubble. Remove from oven and add your preferred pizza toppings, then return to oven 5–8 minutes or until toppings are heated to your preference.

BROWN SUGAR SCONES WITH FRESH BERRIES

PREP TIME: 30 MIN | COOK TIME: 15 MIN | YIELDS 4 SCONES

Dark brown sugar gives these scones a rich, almost molasses flavor, which pairs well with fresh berries. If fresh berries are not in season feel free to use unsweetened frozen berries that have been thawed and drained of excess juices.

INGREDIENTS

⅔ cup all-purpose flour

½ teaspoon baking powder

3 tablespoons dark brown sugar, divided

⅛ teaspoon salt

2 tablespoons cubed salted butter, chilled

⅓ cup fresh blueberries

¼ cup cold heavy cream

1 large egg yolk

1. Preheat oven to 350°F and line a baking sheet with parchment or a reusable silicone baking mat.

2. In a medium bowl, combine flour, baking powder, 2 tablespoons brown sugar, and salt. Whisk well to combine. Add butter and use your fingers to rub mixture until butter is in pea-sized pieces and flour resembles coarse sand. Toss in blueberries and mix well. Cover and chill 10 minutes.

3. Make a well in dry ingredients and add cream and egg yolk. Gently whisk egg yolk with cream, then stir in flour until it just forms a shaggy ball. Turn out onto a lightly floured surface and press dough into a ½"-thick rectangle, then fold dough in half. Turn dough a quarter turn and repeat this process three more times. You may need to use a spatula or bench scraper the first few times, as the dough will be shaggy. Cover dough and chill 10 minutes.

4. Once chilled, use your hands to form dough into a ¾"-thick circle. Use a sharp chef's knife to cut dough into four wedges by pressing straight down and lifting straight up. Transfer wedges to prepared baking sheet. Top each with a sprinkle of remaining 1 tablespoon brown sugar.

5. Bake 15–18 minutes or until scones are puffed and golden brown. Cool on the baking sheet 5 minutes before enjoying.

PIGS IN BISCUITS

PREP TIME: 30 MIN | COOK TIME: 8 MIN | YIELDS 6 BISCUITS

This variation of the traditional pigs in a blanket uses fluffy biscuit dough in place of the traditional yeast dough and is a great meal or snack (think the big game). Make these up the evening before, and you can cook them straight from the refrigerator for breakfast the next day. You can also make these with hot dogs for a lunch-sized meal!

INGREDIENTS

¼ cup all-purpose flour

¼ teaspoon baking powder

¼ teaspoon granulated sugar

2 tablespoons cubed salted butter, chilled

1 tablespoon plus 1 teaspoon cold buttermilk

6 cocktail-sized sausages, dried well

1. Preheat oven to 350°F and line a baking sheet with parchment or a reusable silicone baking mat.

2. In a medium bowl, combine flour, baking powder, and sugar. Whisk well to combine. Add butter and use your fingers to rub mixture until butter is in pea-sized pieces and flour resembles coarse sand. Cover and chill 10 minutes.

3. Make a well in dry ingredients and add buttermilk. Gently stir until it just forms a shaggy ball. Turn out onto a lightly floured surface and press dough into a ¼"-thick rectangle, then fold dough in half. Turn dough a quarter turn and repeat this process four more times. You may need to use a spatula or bench scraper the first few times, as the dough will be shaggy. Cover dough and chill 10 minutes.

4. Once chilled, use your hands to form dough into a ¼"-thick rectangle. Use a sharp chef's knife to cut dough into six strips by pressing straight down and lifting straight up.

5. Wrap each biscuit strip around a sausage and place them seam-side down on prepared baking sheet.

6. Bake 8–11 minutes or until biscuits are puffed and golden brown and sausages are hot. Cool on the baking sheet 5 minutes before enjoying.

SMALL-BATCH PAIN AU CHOCOLAT

PREP TIME: 3 HOURS | COOK TIME: 13 MIN | YIELDS 4 ROLLS

Translating to "chocolate bread," *pain au chocolat* is a popular French pastry that combines a buttery, flaky roll with rich, semisweet chocolate. This recipe takes a few shortcuts from the more complicated original, but the results are just as delicious! If you are making these on a warm day you may want to chill them a little longer between folds to keep your butter cold.

INGREDIENTS

¼ cup water

1 tablespoon granulated sugar

½ teaspoon dry active yeast

1 large egg yolk

2 tablespoons unsalted butter, melted and cooled

¼ teaspoon salt

½ cup all-purpose flour

½ cup bread flour

¼ cup unsalted butter, at room temperature

2 ounces coarsely chopped semisweet chocolate

1 tablespoon heavy cream

1 In a small microwave-safe bowl, heat water 20 seconds or until it reaches 110°F. Stir in sugar and yeast and allow to stand until yeast is bubbling and foamy, about 10 minutes.

2 To the work bowl of a stand mixer fitted with a dough hook, or in a large bowl using a wooden spoon, add yeast mixture, egg yolk, and melted butter. Mix on medium speed until well combined, then add salt and both flours and mix on low speed for 1 minute. Increase speed to medium and knead 4 minutes or until dough is smooth. If mixing by hand, use the spoon to stir in flour until it forms a shaggy ball, then knead in the bowl by hand until dough is smooth, about 10 minutes.

3 Form dough into a smooth ball, then cover bowl with a damp towel and let rise in a draft-free spot 1 hour or until doubled in bulk.

4 Line a ¼ sheet pan or 8" × 8" cake pan with parchment.

5 Turn dough out onto a lightly floured surface. Press out any air bubbles with your palm. Roll dough into a ¼"-thick 6" × 3" rectangle. Spread room-temperature butter over dough, then fold the short sides of the dough into the center like folding a letter, wrap in plastic, and chill 30 minutes.

6. After 30 minutes, remove dough from refrigerator to a lightly floured surface with the long side facing you. Roll dough out to a ¼"-thick 6" × 3" rectangle and repeat the folds as before. Cover and return to refrigerator 15 minutes.

7. Once chilled, roll dough out into a ¼"-thick 6" × 3" rectangle. Cut dough into four rectangles, divide chocolate along short side of rectangles, then roll dough over chocolate. Transfer to prepared sheet pan, cover with a damp towel, and allow to rise 30 minutes or until rolls are puffy and a finger pressed into the side leaves a mark.

8. Preheat oven to 400°F.

9. Once risen, brush rolls with cream, then bake 12–15 minutes or until rolls are golden brown on top and bottom and puffed. Cool on the baking sheet 10 minutes before serving.

EASY BUTTERMILK DROP BISCUITS

PREP TIME: 10 MIN | COOK TIME: 18 MIN | YIELDS 4 BISCUITS

Drop biscuits are among the easiest biscuits going. Simply mix, scoop, and bake, and in less than 30 minutes you have hot biscuits ready for whatever meal you are making. To make these extra rich, brush them with a little melted butter when they are fresh from the oven!

INGREDIENTS

½ cup all-purpose flour

¼ teaspoon baking powder

⅛ teaspoon baking soda

½ teaspoon granulated sugar

⅛ teaspoon salt

2 tablespoons cubed salted butter, chilled

¼ cup plus 1 tablespoon buttermilk

1. Preheat oven to 350°F and line a baking sheet with parchment or a reusable silicone baking mat.

2. In a medium bowl, combine flour, baking powder, baking soda, sugar, and salt. Whisk well to combine. Add butter and use your fingers to rub mixture until it resembles coarse sand.

3. Make a well in dry ingredients and add buttermilk. Gently stir until a shaggy dough forms and no dry flour remains.

4. Scoop dough onto prepared baking sheet in four equal mounds. Bake 18–20 minutes or until biscuits are puffed and golden brown. Cool on the baking sheet 3 minutes before enjoying.

Drop Biscuit Variations

Drop biscuits are versatile. You can make them into beer cheese biscuits by swapping 2 tablespoons of buttermilk for a lager-style beer, and adding ⅓ cup coarsely shredded sharp Cheddar with the wet ingredients. You can also make sweet blueberry maple biscuits by swapping 1 tablespoon buttermilk for 1 tablespoon maple syrup and folding in ⅓ cup fresh or frozen blueberries. Use your imagination and enjoy!

EASY BISCUIT CINNAMON ROLLS

PREP TIME: 30 MIN | COOK TIME: 15 MIN | YIELDS 2 ROLLS

These cinnamon rolls are tender and sweet, and they satisfy any cinnamon roll craving without having to wait for yeast to activate, dough to proof, and rolls to rise.

INGREDIENTS

¼ cup plus 1 teaspoon all-purpose flour

¼ cup plus 1 teaspoon bread flour

½ teaspoon baking powder

1 teaspoon granulated sugar

3 tablespoons cubed salted butter, chilled

¼ cup cold buttermilk

¼ teaspoon pure vanilla extract

2 tablespoons salted butter, at room temperature

2 tablespoons packed light brown sugar

¼ teaspoon ground cinnamon

1. Preheat oven to 350°F and line a baking sheet with parchment or a reusable silicone baking mat.

2. In a medium bowl, combine flours, baking powder, and granulated sugar. Whisk well to combine. Add chilled butter and use your fingers to rub mixture until butter is in pea-sized pieces and flour resembles coarse sand. Cover and chill 10 minutes.

3. Make a well in dry ingredients and add buttermilk and vanilla. Gently stir until it just forms a shaggy ball. Turn out onto a lightly floured surface and press dough into a ½"-thick rectangle, then fold dough in half. Turn dough a quarter turn and repeat this process four more times. You may need to use a spatula the first few times, as dough will be shaggy. Cover dough and chill 10 minutes.

4. In a small bowl, combine room-temperature butter, brown sugar, and cinnamon. Mix until smooth.

5. Once chilled, use your hands to form dough into a ½"-thick rectangle. Spread cinnamon filling over dough, then roll dough along the short side into a log. Use a sharp chef's knife to cut dough in half by pressing straight down and lifting straight up. This will help your layers to stay separate. Transfer rolls to prepared baking sheet.

6. Bake 15–18 minutes or until rolls are puffed and golden brown and cinnamon filling is bubbling. Cool on the baking sheet 5 minutes before enjoying.

CHAPTER 5
PIES, TARTS, AND COBBLERS

Pies, tarts, and cobblers are some of the most beloved comfort foods. They can be sweet or savory, they can be enjoyed at almost any occasion, and they can right the wrongs of the day. The only problem with them is they are best when they are fresh, meaning the day they are made. No one wants soggy pie or stale cobbler, but a full-sized recipe will leave you with just that. The solution can be found ahead!

In this chapter you will find recipes to make petite versions of the classics sized just right for one person to enjoy. You will also find recipes to make pastry and cookie crusts, so your pies will have the perfect homemade base. You will find seasonal favorites like Classic Apple Pie and Pecan Pie, savory pies like Ham and Cheddar Quiche for One, and unique recipes like Chocolate Cobbler and Peanut Butter Fluff Pie. Throughout the chapter, there are additional tips and tricks to help you bake with success and less waste. So, enjoy your pie, cobbler, or tart—and enjoy all of it too!

PERSONAL-SIZED PASTRY CRUST

PREP TIME: 40 MIN | COOK TIME: 0 MIN | YIELDS 1 (6") CRUST

Pastry pie crusts are a classic, and are what most people think of when pie is mentioned. This crust can easily be doubled for a double-crust pie. It is extremely versatile and can be used for sweet and savory dishes, so you can use the same recipe for fruit pies, cream pies, pot pies, and quiche!

INGREDIENTS

½ cup all-purpose flour

½ teaspoon granulated sugar

3 tablespoons cubed salted butter, chilled

1 tablespoon ice water

1 In a medium bowl, combine flour and sugar. Whisk well to combine.

2 Add butter to flour and use your fingers to work butter into flour until it resembles coarse sand with a few pea-sized pieces.

3 Add water and mix with your fingers until dough starts to clump. If needed, add more water 1 teaspoon at a time until dough comes together and no dry flour remains.

4 Turn dough out onto a lightly floured surface and flatten dough with your palm into a fat disk. Fold dough in half and press dough out again. Rotate dough a quarter turn and repeat folding and pressing twice more. Wrap dough in plastic and chill 30 minutes or up to overnight.

5 When ready to use, pull dough from refrigerator and let it warm up 10 minutes before rolling it out on a lightly floured surface as directed for your recipe.

Blind Baking

If your recipe calls for a baked pastry crust you will need to do the following. First, slip crust into a pie or tart pan. Be sure to let the crust slip into the pan; do not tug or pull. Next, line the inside of the crust with aluminum foil, then fill with uncooked rice or dried beans. Bake at 350°F for 10 minutes, then carefully remove foil and beans or rice. Return to the oven and bake 10–15 minutes more or until crust is golden brown all over and crisp. Cool completely before filling.

COOKIE CRUST FOR ONE

PREP TIME: 10 MIN | COOK TIME: 8 MIN | YIELDS 1 (6") CRUST

You can make this crust with any kind of crisp cookies or graham crackers that you like. You can also make this with finely crushed pretzels for a sweet and savory twist on a traditional crust perfect for cream and mousse pies.

INGREDIENTS

½ cup finely ground cookie crumbs

2 tablespoons salted butter, melted

1 tablespoon granulated sugar

1. Preheat oven to 350°F.
2. In a medium bowl, combine all ingredients and mix until crumbs are evenly coated in butter.
3. Transfer crumbs to a 6" pie or tart pan and press crumbs into pan so bottom and sides are packed in evenly and firmly.
4. Bake 8 minutes or until crust is golden brown and smelling toasty. Cool to room temperature before filling.

KEY LIME PIE

PREP TIME: 4½ HOURS | COOK TIME: 10 MIN | YIELDS 1 (6") PIE

Key limes are small, so it takes quite a few to get a substantial amount of juice, but the work is worth it. If you want a shortcut, you can purchase bottled key lime juice in most grocery stores.

INGREDIENTS

2 large egg yolks

3 tablespoons key lime juice

¼ cup sweetened condensed milk

⅛ teaspoon pure vanilla extract

1 Cookie Crust for One, baked and cooled (see recipe in this chapter)

1. Preheat oven to 350°F.
2. In a medium bowl, whisk egg yolks to break, then add lime juice, condensed milk, and vanilla. Mix until smooth.
3. Pour filling into prepared Cookie Crust for One. Bake 10 minutes. Remove from oven and cool 20 minutes at room temperature before refrigerating 4 hours. Serve chilled.

CLASSIC APPLE PIE

PREP TIME: 30 MIN | COOK TIME: 46 MIN | YIELDS 1 (6") PIE

Firm apples are best for baked apple pies. Granny Smith apples make a tarter pie filling, while Fuji and Pink Lady are more balanced in flavor.

INGREDIENTS

2 Personal-Sized Pastry Crusts, unbaked, divided (see recipe in this chapter)

2 medium-sized firm baking apples, peeled, cored, and sliced

1 tablespoon granulated sugar

½ tablespoon unsalted butter

¼ teaspoon ground cinnamon

⅛ teaspoon allspice

1 teaspoon water

½ teaspoon cornstarch

½ teaspoon lemon juice

1 tablespoon whole milk

1. Roll out half Personal-Sized Pastry Crust on a lightly floured surface until it forms an 8" circle. Slide dough into a 6" pie pan. Cover with plastic wrap and refrigerate until ready to use.

2. Roll out remaining half crust on a lightly floured surface until it forms a 7" circle. Slide crust onto a large plate. Cover with plastic wrap and refrigerate.

3. Preheat oven to 400°F and place a baking sheet on bottom rack of oven.

4. In a medium skillet, add apples, sugar, butter, cinnamon, and allspice. Heat over medium heat until butter melts, then cook, stirring often, until apples are tender, about 5 minutes.

5. Reduce heat to low. In a small bowl, add water and cornstarch and mix to form a slurry. Add slurry to apples and mix well. Cook until mixture thickens, about 1 minute. Add lemon juice and stir well. Remove from heat and cool 10 minutes.

6. Remove pie crusts from refrigerator. Spread apple mixture evenly into pastry-lined pie pan. Place top crust over apples. Trim dough to ½" of pan's edge. Tuck edge of top crust under edge of bottom crust. Crimp dough using your fingers or a fork.

7. Cut four ½" vents into pie. Brush with milk, then bake 5 minutes. Reduce heat to 350°F and bake 35–40 minutes or until crust is golden brown.

8. Remove pie from oven and let cool 1 hour before enjoying.

FRESH STRAWBERRY PIE

PREP TIME: 1½ HOURS | COOK TIME: 2 MIN | YIELDS 1 (6") PIE

When strawberries are in season this pie is the perfect way to celebrate them. The traditional strawberry pie is often made with strawberry gelatin, but for this dish, fresh berries are puréed and then thickened with cornstarch so the flavor of the fresh berries is allowed to shine.

INGREDIENTS

1 cup hulled fresh strawberries, sliced in half, divided

¼ cup granulated sugar

¼ cup water, divided

1 tablespoon cornstarch

½ teaspoon pure vanilla extract, divided

1 Personal-Sized Pastry Crust, baked and cooled (see recipe in this chapter)

¼ cup heavy whipping cream

1 tablespoon powdered sugar

1. In a blender, add ¼ cup strawberries, granulated sugar, and 2 tablespoons water. Purée until smooth, then strain mixture through a fine-mesh strainer into a medium saucepan.

2. Place the saucepan over medium heat and cook puréed strawberry mixture until sugar dissolves, about 1 minute.

3. In a small bowl, add remaining 2 tablespoons water and cornstarch and stir to make a slurry. Pour slurry into strawberry purée and stir to mix. Cook until mixture thickens, about 30 seconds. Remove from heat and stir in ¼ teaspoon vanilla. Stir in remaining ¾ cup berries.

4. Pour strawberries into Personal-Sized Pastry Crust. Place in refrigerator at least 1 hour or until filling is chilled thoroughly.

5. Once pie is chilled, in a medium bowl, add cream, powdered sugar, and remaining ¼ teaspoon vanilla. Whip on medium speed until soft peaks form, about 2 minutes. Spread whipped cream over pie. Serve immediately.

Hulling Strawberries

To hull fresh strawberries, insert the tip of a sharp paring knife into the top of the strawberry next to the stem cap at a 45-degree angle toward the center of the berry. Cut around the green top and gently lift the top from the berry; discard.

TOASTED COCONUT CREAM PIE

PREP TIME: 4½ HOURS | COOK TIME: 15 MIN | YIELDS 1 (6") PIE

Full-fat coconut milk provides an additional layer of coconut flavor to this pie, but if you do not have any, you can use 1 full cup of half-and-half. Toasting the coconut adds a special touch to this pie but is unnecessary if you prefer to skip this step. Graham cracker crumbs are perfect for the crust of this pie.

INGREDIENTS

⅓ cup shredded sweetened coconut, divided

½ cup full-fat canned coconut milk

½ cup half-and-half

3 tablespoons granulated sugar

1 tablespoon cornstarch

1 large egg yolk

1 tablespoon unsalted butter

½ teaspoon pure vanilla extract, divided

1 Cookie Crust for One, baked and cooled (see recipe in this chapter)

¼ cup heavy whipping cream

1 tablespoon powdered sugar

1. In a small skillet over medium-low heat, add coconut. Cook, stirring constantly, until coconut just starts to turn golden, 4–6 minutes. Remove skillet from heat and continue to stir 1 minute to prevent burning. Set aside.

2. In a medium saucepan over medium-low heat, whisk together coconut milk, half-and-half, sugar, cornstarch, and egg yolk. Whisk until mixture starts to steam, about 4 minutes. Continue to whisk constantly until mixture thickens and starts to simmer, about 6 minutes. Cook 15 seconds, then remove from heat and stir in ¼ cup toasted coconut, butter, and ¼ teaspoon vanilla. Mix well.

3. Pour mixture into prepared Cookie Crust for One. Place a layer of plastic wrap directly on filling and chill 4 hours or overnight.

4. Once chilled, in medium bowl, add cream, powdered sugar, and remaining ¼ teaspoon vanilla. Whip on medium speed until soft peaks form, about 2 minutes.

5. Spread cream over pie and garnish with remaining toasted coconut. Serve immediately or chill up to 1 hour.

CARAMEL APPLE PIE

PREP TIME: 30 MIN | COOK TIME: 46 MIN | YIELDS 1 (6") PIE

This crumble-topped pie has all the best flavors of a caramel apple baked into an irresistible pie. This is at its most delicious when served warm with a scoop of cool vanilla ice cream!

INGREDIENTS

1 Personal-Sized Pastry Crust, unbaked (see recipe in this chapter)

2 tablespoons all-purpose flour

2 tablespoons packed light brown sugar

1½ tablespoons unsalted butter, divided

2 medium-sized firm baking apples, peeled, cored, and sliced

1 tablespoon granulated sugar

¼ teaspoon ground cinnamon

1 teaspoon water

½ teaspoon cornstarch

4 caramel candies, cut in half

1. Roll out Personal-Sized Pastry Crust on a lightly floured surface until it forms an 8" circle. Slide dough into a 6" pie pan, making sure not to stretch or tug. Cover with plastic wrap and refrigerate.

2. In a small bowl, combine flour and brown sugar. Mix well, then add 1 tablespoon butter and use your fingers to rub butter into flour until it forms a crumble. Cover with plastic wrap and refrigerate.

3. Preheat oven to 400°F and place a baking sheet on bottom rack of oven.

4. In a medium skillet, add apples, granulated sugar, remaining ½ tablespoon butter, and cinnamon. Heat over medium heat until butter melts, then cook, stirring often, until apples are tender, about 5 minutes.

5. Reduce heat to low. In a small bowl, add water and cornstarch and mix to form a slurry. Add to apples and mix. Cook until mixture thickens, about 1 minute. Remove from heat and cool 10 minutes.

6. Remove pie crust and crumble from refrigerator. Spread half of the apple mixture evenly into pastry-lined pie pan and top with caramels. Cover with remaining apples, then top with crumble.

7. Bake on heated baking sheet 5 minutes, then reduce heat to 350°F and bake another 35–40 minutes or until crumble is golden brown.

8. Let cool 1 hour before enjoying.

PUMPKIN PIE

PREP TIME: 10 MIN | COOK TIME: 35 MIN | YIELDS 1 (6") PIE

Pumpkin pie is a fall classic and is perfect when there is a chill in the air. For this recipe, be sure you purchase pure pumpkin purée, not pumpkin pie filling, which has sugar and spices added. Leftover pumpkin purée can be used in smoothies, soups, or made into Pumpkin Bread (see Chapter 7).

INGREDIENTS

1 Personal-Sized Pastry Crust, unbaked (see recipe in this chapter)

3 tablespoons granulated sugar

¼ teaspoon ground cinnamon

⅛ teaspoon ground allspice

⅛ teaspoon ground cloves

1 pinch (about ¹⁄₁₆ teaspoon) ground nutmeg

1 large egg yolk

¾ cup pumpkin purée

¼ cup heavy cream

1. Preheat oven to 400°F.

2. Roll out Personal-Sized Pastry Crust on a lightly floured surface until it forms an 8" circle. Slide dough into a 6" pie pan, making sure not to stretch or tug. Cover with plastic wrap and refrigerate until ready to use.

3. In a medium bowl, whisk together sugar, cinnamon, allspice, cloves, and nutmeg until well combined.

4. Add egg yolk, pumpkin, and cream and whisk until smooth.

5. Pour mixture into prepared crust and place on a baking sheet. Bake in lower third of oven 10 minutes, then reduce heat to 350°F and bake an additional 25–30 minutes or until filling is set at the edges and slightly wobbly in the center.

6. Cool 3 hours on a wire rack before enjoying.

Quick Pumpkin Bisque

You can use leftover pumpkin purée to make a delicious soup. In a medium saucepan over medium heat, add 1 tablespoon salted butter. Once melted, about 20 seconds, add ¼ chopped onion and cook until soft, about 2 minutes. Add ¼ teaspoon ground cinnamon and ⅛ teaspoon each ground cumin and ground coriander. Sauté for 30 seconds, then add 1 cup vegetable broth and 1 cup pumpkin purée. Mix until well combined, then simmer for 20 minutes. Transfer mixture to a blender and purée until smooth, then stir in 3 tablespoons heavy cream. Serve hot.

VERY BERRY POCKET PIE

PREP TIME: 10 MIN | COOK TIME: 20 MIN | YIELDS 1 (5") PIE

Pocket pies are also called hand pies because they can be eaten out of hand, no plates or forks required. It may feel decadent, but this pie makes an excellent breakfast when you are looking for a fun treat to start your day. Use any mix of berries that are freshest in the market.

INGREDIENTS

½ cup mixed fresh berries

2 tablespoons granulated sugar

2 teaspoons cornstarch

½ teaspoon freshly grated lemon zest

1 Personal-Sized Pastry Crust, unbaked (see recipe in this chapter)

1 tablespoon whole milk

1. Preheat oven to 350°F and line a baking sheet with parchment or a reusable silicone baking mat.

2. In a medium bowl, combine berries, sugar, cornstarch, and lemon zest. Toss to combine. Set aside.

3. Roll out Personal-Sized Pastry Crust on a lightly floured surface until it forms an 8" circle and place on prepared baking sheet.

4. Add berry mixture to center of crust. Brush milk around edge of crust, fold in half, then crimp dough with your fingers or the tines of a fork. With a paring knife, cut two small slits into top of pie, then brush lightly with milk.

5. Bake 20–25 minutes or until pie is golden brown and filling is bubbling. Cool on the baking sheet at least 20 minutes before serving.

PEANUT BUTTER FLUFF PIE

PREP TIME: 2½ HOURS | COOK TIME: 0 MIN | YIELDS 1 (6") PIE

This pie is sweet and tangy with a rich peanut butter flavor. It pairs well with a cup of strong coffee or a shot of espresso. To ramp up the peanut butter flavor you can use finely crushed peanut butter cookies for the crust, such as the Classic Peanut Butter Cookies in Chapter 2.

INGREDIENTS

3 tablespoons creamy peanut butter

1 ounce cream cheese, at room temperature

¼ cup powdered sugar, divided

¼ cup heavy whipping cream

¼ teaspoon pure vanilla extract

1 Cookie Crust for One, baked and cooled (see recipe in this chapter)

2 tablespoons hot fudge sauce

1 tablespoon peanut pieces

1. In a medium bowl, combine peanut butter and cream cheese. Use a hand mixer on low speed to cream together until smooth, about 30 seconds. Add 2 tablespoons powdered sugar and beat on low speed for 10 seconds, then increase speed to high and beat until light and fluffy, about 2 minutes. Set aside.

2. In a separate medium bowl, add 2 tablespoons powdered sugar, cream, and vanilla. Beat on low speed 30 seconds, then increase speed to high and beat until cream forms soft peaks, about 1 minute.

3. Add whipped cream to peanut butter mixture and beat on medium speed until thoroughly mixed and fluffy, about 20 seconds.

4. Spread filling inside prepared Cookie Crust for One. Cover loosely with plastic wrap and refrigerate 2 hours.

5. To serve, garnish with hot fudge sauce and peanuts and serve immediately.

Hot Fudge Sauce for One

Homemade hot fudge sauce is easy to make, and it tastes so much better than store-bought. To make enough for one, combine 3 tablespoons heavy cream, 2 tablespoons granulated sugar, 1 tablespoon unsalted butter, and 1 teaspoon corn syrup in a small saucepan. Bring to a boil over medium heat and stir to melt butter and sugar. Allow to boil for 1 minute, then remove from heat and stir in 1½ ounces chopped semisweet chocolate and ¼ teaspoon vanilla extract until smooth. Use immediately or store in the refrigerator and reheat in the microwave before serving.

APPLE CINNAMON POCKET PIE

PREP TIME: 10 MIN | COOK TIME: 20 MIN | YIELDS 1 (5") PIE

For a sparkly decorative flourish you can sprinkle the top of this pie with a little coarse sanding sugar and a pinch of additional cinnamon. The coarse sugar will not fully melt, leaving the crust with a pretty, glittery finish.

INGREDIENTS

½ cup chopped apple

2 tablespoons packed light brown sugar

2 teaspoons cornstarch

¼ teaspoon ground cinnamon

1 Personal-Sized Pastry Crust, unbaked (see recipe in this chapter)

1 tablespoon whole milk

1. Preheat oven to 350°F and line a baking sheet with parchment or a reusable silicone baking mat.

2. In a medium bowl, combine apples, brown sugar, cornstarch, and cinnamon. Toss to combine. Set aside.

3. Roll out Personal-Sized Pastry Crust on a lightly floured surface until it forms an 8" circle and place on prepared baking sheet.

4. Add apple mixture to center of crust. Brush milk around edge of crust, fold in half, then crimp dough with your fingers or the tines of a fork. With a paring knife, cut two small slits into top of pie, then brush lightly with milk.

5. Bake 20–25 minutes or until pie is golden brown and filling is bubbling. Cool on the baking sheet at least 20 minutes before serving.

Store-Bought Pastry Crust
Sometimes you want a pie without the hassle of making a crust from scratch. When that happens, you can use ready-made pastry crusts from the refrigerated section of the grocery store. One-third of a crust should be enough for most single-serving recipes. Simply fold the corners into the center of the wedge, then roll on a lightly floured surface until crust is 8" in diameter. The leftover crust can be chilled up to a week, and the unused crust can be frozen, then thawed overnight for use another time.

CHERRY ALMOND POCKET PIE

Almond extract is powerful stuff, and just a little will go a long way, so while ⅛ teaspoon may not seem like much, it is more than enough to flavor this pie. If you also want the crunch of almond in the pie you can add 2 tablespoons of toasted slivered almonds to the filling along with the vanilla and almond extracts.

INGREDIENTS

½ cup frozen dark sweet cherries, thawed, juices reserved

2 tablespoons packed light brown sugar

2 teaspoons cornstarch

⅛ teaspoon ground cinnamon

¼ teaspoon pure vanilla extract

⅛ teaspoon almond extract

1 Personal-Sized Pastry Crust, unbaked (see recipe in this chapter)

1 tablespoon whole milk

1. In a medium saucepan, combine cherries with their juice, brown sugar, cornstarch, and cinnamon. Cook over medium heat until mixture thickens, about 3 minutes. Remove from heat and stir in vanilla and almond extract. Cool to room temperature.

2. Preheat oven to 350°F and line a baking sheet with parchment or a reusable silicone baking mat.

3. Roll out Personal-Sized Pastry Crust on a lightly floured surface until it forms an 8" circle and place on prepared baking sheet.

4. Add cherry mixture to center of crust. Brush milk around edge of crust, fold in half, then crimp dough with your fingers or the tines of a fork. With a paring knife, cut two small slits into top of pie, then brush lightly with milk.

5. Bake 20–25 minutes or until pie is golden brown and filling is bubbling. Cool on the baking sheet at least 20 minutes before serving.

CARAMEL CUSTARD PIE

PREP TIME: 15 MIN | COOK TIME: 45 MIN | YIELDS 1 (6") PIE

The caramel flavor in this pie comes from boiling the butter and light brown sugar. While this mixture cooks, the butterfat will brown, adding a rich layer of additional flavor to the filling. This step may seem a little fussy, but it is worth it, so don't skip it!

INGREDIENTS

1 Personal-Sized Pastry Crust, unbaked (see recipe in this chapter)

¼ cup packed light brown sugar

3 tablespoons salted butter

1 large egg

⅓ cup evaporated milk

2 teaspoons all-purpose flour

¼ teaspoon pure vanilla extract

1. Preheat oven to 400°F.

2. Roll out Personal-Sized Pastry Crust on a lightly floured surface until it forms an 8" circle. Slide dough into a 6" pie pan, making sure not to stretch or tug. Cover with plastic wrap and refrigerate until ready to use.

3. In a medium saucepan over medium heat, combine brown sugar and butter. Bring to a boil and cook, stirring frequently, 5 minutes or until butter smells nutty. Cool 2 minutes.

4. In a medium bowl, add egg, milk, flour, and vanilla. Whisk until smooth. Slowly whisk in the cooled sugar mixture and whisk until smooth.

5. Pour pie filling into prepared crust and tap gently to release any air bubbles.

6. Bake 5 minutes, then turn oven down to 325°F and bake 35–40 minutes or until pie is golden brown and set throughout.

7. Cool completely before serving.

CHOCOLATE CHIP COOKIE PIE

PREP TIME: 10 MIN | COOK TIME: 35 MIN | YIELDS 1 (6") PIE

If you enjoy ooey-gooey chocolate chip cookies then you will love this pie. It has all the flavors found in traditional chocolate chip cookies baked into a decadent pie. This pie is delicious when it is still slightly warm and served with ice cream or whipped cream.

INGREDIENTS

1 Personal-Sized Pastry Crust, unbaked (see recipe in this chapter)

1 large egg

1 tablespoon all-purpose flour

1 tablespoon granulated sugar

3 tablespoons packed light brown sugar

3 tablespoons salted butter, melted and cooled

¼ teaspoon pure vanilla extract

½ cup semisweet chocolate chips

1 Preheat oven to 325°F.

2 Roll out Personal-Sized Pastry Crust on a lightly floured surface until it forms an 8" circle. Slide dough into a 6" pie pan, making sure not to stretch or tug. Cover with plastic wrap and refrigerate until ready to use.

3 In a medium bowl, add egg, flour, granulated sugar, brown sugar, butter, and vanilla. Whisk to combine. Add chocolate chips and stir to mix.

4 Pour pie filling into prepared crust and tap gently to release any air bubbles.

5 Bake 35–40 minutes or until pie is golden brown and puffed around edges but still slightly wobbly in center.

6 Cool completely before serving.

BLUEBERRY CRUMBLE PIE

PREP TIME: 15 MIN | COOK TIME: 40 MIN | YIELDS 1 (6") PIE

If you are using frozen blueberries for this pie, it is best to thaw them and drain off the excess juices so the pie won't be too watery. This is a good idea when using any frozen fruits for pies, tarts, and crumbles. Save the juices for smoothies!

INGREDIENTS

1 Personal-Sized Pastry Crust, unbaked (see recipe in this chapter)

2 tablespoons all-purpose flour

2 tablespoons packed light brown sugar

1 tablespoon unsalted butter

1¼ cups fresh blueberries

1 tablespoon plus 2 teaspoons granulated sugar

1 tablespoon cornstarch

½ teaspoon freshly grated lemon zest

1. Preheat oven to 400°F and place a baking sheet on bottom rack of oven.

2. Roll out Personal-Sized Pastry Crust on a lightly floured surface until it forms an 8" circle. Slide dough into a 6" pie pan, making sure not to stretch or tug. Cover with plastic wrap and refrigerate until ready to use.

3. In a small bowl, combine flour and brown sugar. Mix well, then add butter and use your fingers to rub butter into flour until it forms a crumble. Cover with plastic wrap and refrigerate until ready to use.

4. In a medium bowl, combine blueberries, granulated sugar, cornstarch, and lemon zest. Mix well. Pour blueberry mixture into prepared crust. Sprinkle crumble topping over top.

5. Bake on heated baking sheet 5 minutes, then reduce heat to 350°F and bake another 35–40 minutes or until crumble is golden brown and filling is bubbling.

6. Remove pie from oven and let cool 1 hour before enjoying.

Streusel, Crumble, and Crisp

Ever wondered what the difference is between a crumble, crisp, and streusel? Streusel can be either a crisp or a crumble; it is any topping made with butter, flour, sugar, and other ingredients. A crisp is a bit denser and is simply butter, flour, and sugar mixed until clumps form. A crisp contains the same ingredients but adds old-fashioned oats, which get crisp while baking.

CHESS PIE

This pie, thought to have English origins, is now a staple of the American South. Don't be deceived by the simple ingredients. The rich custard filling is sweet and a little gooey, much like a pecan pie, and this version is flavored with vanilla and lemon.

INGREDIENTS

1 Personal-Sized Pastry Crust, unbaked (see recipe in this chapter)

1 large egg

2 tablespoons salted butter, melted and cooled

¼ cup granulated sugar

1 teaspoon yellow cornmeal

2 tablespoons whole milk

1 teaspoon lemon juice

¼ teaspoon pure vanilla extract

1. Preheat oven to 350°F.

2. Roll out Personal-Sized Pastry Crust on a lightly floured surface until it forms an 8" circle. Slide dough into a 6" pie pan, making sure not to stretch or tug. Cover with plastic wrap and refrigerate until ready to use.

3. In a medium bowl, add egg, butter, sugar, cornmeal, milk, lemon juice, and vanilla. Whisk until smooth.

4. Pour pie filling into prepared crust and tap gently to release any air bubbles.

5. Bake 35–40 minutes or until pie is golden brown and set throughout.

6. Cool completely before serving.

FRESH PEACH GALETTE

PREP TIME: 20 MIN | COOK TIME: 20 MIN | YIELDS 1 (5") TART

A galette is a rustic tart that does not require any special baking tools or skills. This galette will become a summer favorite when peach season is at its peak. The galette is simply begging to be topped with a scoop of vanilla or peach ice cream.

INGREDIENTS

1 Personal-Sized Pastry Crust, unbaked (see recipe in this chapter)

1 large yellow peach, peeled, pitted, and sliced into eight wedges

2 teaspoons packed light brown sugar

1 teaspoon cornstarch

⅛ teaspoon ground cinnamon

1. Preheat oven to 375°F and line a baking sheet with parchment or a reusable silicone baking mat.

2. Roll out Personal-Sized Pastry Crust on a lightly floured surface until it forms an 8" circle and place on prepared baking sheet.

3. In a medium bowl, add peach slices, brown sugar, cornstarch, and cinnamon. Toss to coat peach slices evenly.

4. Arrange peach slices in center of pastry crust, leaving a 1" border around the edge of peaches. Fold pastry crust over the edges of peach slices.

5. Bake 20–25 minutes or until peaches are tender and crust is golden brown. Cool 10 minutes before serving.

SINGLE-SERVING PEACH COBBLER

PREP TIME: 15 MIN | COOK TIME: 35 MIN | YIELDS 1 (6") COBBLER

Peach cobbler traditionally has a sweet drop biscuit topping that, when baked, resembles cobblestones. This version adds a little cinnamon to the biscuits to enhance the flavor of the peaches, and to make every bite even more delicious!

INGREDIENTS

¼ cup all-purpose flour

2 tablespoons granulated sugar, divided

¼ teaspoon baking powder

⅛ teaspoon ground cinnamon

1 tablespoon cubed salted butter, chilled

2 tablespoons whole milk

2 medium peaches, peeled, pitted, and sliced

2 tablespoons packed light brown sugar

1 tablespoon cornstarch

¼ teaspoon pure vanilla extract

1. Preheat oven to 350°F and place a baking sheet on bottom rack of oven.

2. In a medium bowl, combine flour, 1 tablespoon granulated sugar, baking powder, and cinnamon. Whisk well to combine. Add butter and use your fingers to rub mixture until it resembles coarse sand.

3. Make a well in dry ingredients and add milk. Gently stir until a shaggy batter forms and no dry flour remains. Set aside.

4. In a medium bowl, add peaches, brown sugar, cornstarch, and vanilla. Toss well to coat. Transfer mixture to a 6" pie pan.

5. Dollop biscuit mixture evenly over peaches by heaping teaspoons. Sprinkle with remaining 1 tablespoon granulated sugar.

6. Bake on heated baking sheet 35–40 minutes or until topping is golden brown and filling is bubbling.

7. Remove cobbler from oven and let cool 30 minutes before enjoying.

CHOCOLATE CREAM PIE

PREP TIME: 4½ HOURS | COOK TIME: 11 MIN | YIELDS 1 (6") PIE

If you love chocolate and want to pack in as much chocolate as you can, make this pie with a chocolate cookie crust rather than graham cracker. Dutch-processed cocoa powder makes the flavor of this pie a little more bitter than natural cocoa powder, so if you prefer a sweeter flavor, you can make the switch.

INGREDIENTS

1 cup half-and-half

3 tablespoons granulated sugar

1 tablespoon Dutch-processed cocoa powder

1 tablespoon cornstarch

1 large egg yolk

1 tablespoon unsalted butter

1 tablespoon chopped semisweet chocolate

½ teaspoon pure vanilla extract, divided

1 Cookie Crust for One, baked and cooled (see recipe in this chapter)

¼ cup heavy whipping cream

1 tablespoon powdered sugar

1. In a medium saucepan, whisk together half-and-half, granulated sugar, cocoa powder, cornstarch, and egg yolk. Place pan over medium-low heat and whisk until mixture starts to steam, about 4 minutes. Whisk constantly until mixture thickens and starts to simmer, about 6 minutes. Cook 15 seconds, then remove from heat and stir in butter, chocolate, and ¼ teaspoon vanilla. Mix well.

2. Pour mixture into prepared Cookie Crust for One. Place a layer of plastic wrap directly on filling and chill 4 hours or overnight.

3. Once chilled, in a medium bowl, add cream, powdered sugar, and remaining ¼ teaspoon vanilla. Whip on medium speed until soft peaks form, about 2 minutes.

4. Spread cream over pie. Serve immediately or chill up to 1 hour.

BERRY APPLE CRISP

PREP TIME: 15 MIN | COOK TIME: 35 MIN | YIELDS 1 (6") CRISP

The oats in this topping add a chewy texture, but if you do not have oats, you can omit them or replace them with a tablespoon of finely chopped raw pecans, almonds, or walnuts. A little bit of ground cinnamon—about ⅛ teaspoon—would also be a lovely addition.

INGREDIENTS

2 tablespoons all-purpose flour

1 tablespoon old-fashioned oats

2 tablespoons packed light brown sugar

2 tablespoons unsalted butter

1 cup hulled fresh strawberries, quartered

1 medium-sized firm baking apple, peeled, cored, and cut into ½" pieces

1 tablespoon granulated sugar

1 tablespoon cornstarch

½ teaspoon freshly grated lemon zest

¼ teaspoon pure vanilla extract

1. Preheat oven to 350°F and place a baking sheet on bottom rack of oven.

2. In a small bowl, combine flour, oats, and brown sugar. Mix well, then add butter and use your fingers to rub butter into flour until it forms a crumble. Cover with plastic wrap and refrigerate until ready to use.

3. In a medium bowl, combine strawberries, apple, granulated sugar, cornstarch, lemon zest, and vanilla. Toss until evenly mixed. Transfer to a 6" pie pan and sprinkle crisp topping over top.

4. Bake on heated baking sheet 35–40 minutes or until crisp topping is golden brown and filling is bubbling.

5. Remove crisp from oven and let cool 1 hour before enjoying.

PECAN PIE

PREP TIME: 15 MIN | COOK TIME: 40 MIN | YIELDS 1 (6") PIE

The first printed recipes for pecan pie came out of Texas in the 1870s, but the dish quickly spread across the American South and Midwest, where it became a staple throughout the year, particularly during the fall and winter holidays.

INGREDIENTS

1 Personal-Sized Pastry Crust, unbaked (see recipe in this chapter)

2 tablespoons packed light brown sugar

¼ cup corn syrup

1 large egg

2 teaspoons unsalted butter, melted and cooled

2 teaspoons all-purpose flour

¼ teaspoon pure vanilla extract

¼ cup plus 1 tablespoon chopped pecans

1. Preheat oven to 400°F and place a baking sheet on bottom rack of oven.

2. Roll out Personal-Sized Pastry Crust on a lightly floured surface until it forms an 8" circle. Slide dough into a 6" pie pan, making sure not to stretch or tug. Cover with plastic wrap and refrigerate until ready to use.

3. In a medium bowl, combine brown sugar, corn syrup, egg, butter, flour, and vanilla. Whisk until well incorporated and smooth. Stir in pecans and transfer mixture to prepared crust.

4. Bake on heated baking sheet 5 minutes, then reduce heat to 350°F and bake another 35–40 minutes or until pie has puffed all over and crust is golden brown.

5. Remove pie from oven and let cool completely to room temperature before enjoying.

Pie Crust Browning Too Fast?

If you find your pie crust edges are perfectly cooked before your pie's filling is done, you can wrap the crust edges with a strip of aluminum foil. A single layer is usually enough, but you can use a double layer to provide added shielding. The same applies to a crumble, crisp, or top crust. A layer of foil laid on top will stop excess browning but allow for continued cooking.

HAM AND CHEDDAR QUICHE FOR ONE

PREP TIME: 15 MIN | COOK TIME: 48 MIN | YIELDS 1 (6") QUICHE

Quiche is perfect for breakfast, lunch, or dinner, and pairs well with a mixed green salad or a cup of fresh fruit. You can bake this quiche in advance and reheat it in your oven for 10 minutes at 350°F.

INGREDIENTS

1 Personal-Sized Pastry Crust, unbaked (see recipe in this chapter)

2 large eggs

¼ cup whole milk

3 tablespoons heavy cream

⅛ teaspoon salt

⅛ teaspoon ground nutmeg

¼ cup finely chopped ham

¼ cup shredded Cheddar cheese

1. Preheat oven to 350°F.

2. Roll out Personal-Sized Pastry Crust on a lightly floured surface until it forms an 8" circle. Slide dough into a 6" pie pan, making sure not to stretch or tug.

3. Line inside of crust with baking parchment or aluminum foil, fill with uncooked rice or dried beans, and bake 10 minutes. Remove weights and lining, prick bottom of crust four or five times with a fork, then return to oven another 3 minutes. Remove from oven and cool to room temperature.

4. In a medium bowl, add eggs, milk, cream, salt, and nutmeg. Whisk until well combined.

5. Layer ham and cheese in bottom of par-baked pastry crust. Pour egg mixture over top.

6. Bake 35–40 minutes or until filling is golden brown and puffed all over. Cool 30 minutes before serving. Enjoy warm or at room temperature.

PEACH PIE

PREP TIME: 30 MIN | COOK TIME: 41 MIN | YIELDS 1 (6") PIE

Fruit pies that are first cooked on the stove will yield a thicker filling and will not cause an air gap between the filling and the top crust of the pie. The top crust of this Peach Pie is made into a lattice, but you can make it a double-crust pie if that makes your life easier.

INGREDIENTS

2 Personal-Sized Pastry Crusts, unbaked, divided (see recipe in this chapter)

2 medium peaches, peeled, pitted, and sliced

1 tablespoon packed light brown sugar

½ tablespoon unsalted butter

¼ teaspoon ground cardamom

1 teaspoon water

½ teaspoon cornstarch

¼ teaspoon pure vanilla extract

1 tablespoon whole milk

1. Roll out half of Personal-Sized Pastry Crust on a lightly floured surface until it forms an 8" circle. Slide dough into a 6" pie pan, making sure not to stretch or tug. Cover with plastic wrap and refrigerate until ready to use.

2. Roll out remaining half crust on a lightly floured surface until it forms a 7" circle. Cut circle into seven strips. Slide strips onto a large plate. Cover with plastic wrap and refrigerate until ready to use.

3. Preheat oven to 400°F and place a baking sheet on bottom rack of oven.

4. In a medium skillet, add peaches, brown sugar, butter, and cardamom. Heat over medium heat until butter melts, about 20 seconds, then cook, stirring often, until peaches are tender, about 5 minutes.

5. Reduce heat to low. In a small bowl, add water and cornstarch and mix to form a slurry. Add slurry to peaches and mix well. Cook until mixture thickens, about 1 minute. Turn off heat and add vanilla and stir well. Cool 10 minutes.

6. Remove pie crusts from refrigerator. Spread peach mixture evenly in pastry-lined pie pan. Place four crust strips evenly across top of pie. Pull middle strip toward center and lay one reserved strip across bottom ⅓ of pie. Pull two outside strips down pie and lay another reserved strip across center of pie. Pull outside strips back into place. Pull top of middle strip down and lay final strip across pie. Replace strip.

7. Trim dough to ½" of pan's edge. Tuck edge of top crust under edge of bottom crust. Crimp dough with your fingers or the tines of a fork.

8. Brush pastry lattice with milk, then bake on heated baking sheet 5 minutes. Reduce heat to 350°F and bake another 30–35 minutes or until crust is golden brown and filling is bubbling.

9. Remove pie from oven and let cool 1 hour before enjoying.

SILKY CHOCOLATE GANACHE TART

PREP TIME: 1¼ HOURS | COOK TIME: 11 MIN | YIELDS 1 (6") TART

You can grind whole almonds for this tart in a food processor by pulsing them to fine crumbs. Alternatively, you can use ready-ground almond flour and store any excess in your freezer, where it will keep up to a year.

INGREDIENTS

⅓ cup finely ground almonds

2 tablespoons graham cracker crumbs

2 tablespoons unsalted butter, melted and cooled

1 tablespoon granulated sugar

½ cup heavy cream

3 ounces finely chopped semisweet chocolate

2 tablespoons unsalted butter, at room temperature

¼ teaspoon pure vanilla extract

⅛ teaspoon flaky sea salt

1. Preheat oven to 350°F.

2. In a small bowl, combine almonds, cracker crumbs, melted butter, and sugar. Mix until nuts and cracker crumbs are evenly coated in butter. Transfer to a 6" pie pan and press into pan so bottom and sides are packed in evenly and firmly.

3. Bake 8–10 minutes or until crust is golden brown. Set aside to cool to room temperature.

4. In a small saucepan over medium heat, add cream. Once it just comes to a simmer, about 3 minutes, remove from heat and add chocolate and room-temperature butter. Let stand 1 minute, then whisk until mixture is smooth. Stir in vanilla.

5. Pour ganache into prepared crust. Chill uncovered 1 hour. Garnish with sea salt before serving.

CHOCOLATE FUDGE PIE

PREP TIME: 15 MIN | COOK TIME: 38 MIN | YIELDS 1 (6") PIE

Baked custard pies are a bit richer than other kinds of pies. This chocolate pie is definitely rich and is perfect for people who love chocolate desserts that pack a punch. If you want a mocha fudge pie add ¼ teaspoon of instant espresso powder with the cocoa powder.

INGREDIENTS

1 Personal-Sized Pastry Crust, unbaked (see recipe in this chapter)

1 ounce chopped unsweetened chocolate

1 tablespoon unsalted butter

1 large egg

3 tablespoons packed light brown sugar

¼ cup corn syrup

1 teaspoon cocoa powder

¼ teaspoon pure vanilla extract

1. Preheat oven to 375°F.

2. Roll out Personal-Sized Pastry Crust on a lightly floured surface until it forms an 8" circle. Slide dough into a 6" pie pan, making sure not to stretch or tug.

3. In a small microwave-safe bowl, add chocolate and butter. Heat 30 seconds, stir well, then heat in 15-second intervals, stirring well between each interval, until melted and smooth.

4. In a medium bowl, add melted chocolate mixture along with remaining ingredients. Mix until smooth and fully incorporated.

5. Pour filling mixture into prepared crust. Bake 35–40 minutes or until filling is puffed all over and crust is golden brown. Cool completely to room temperature before serving.

BUTTERSCOTCH PIE

PREP TIME: 4½ HOURS | COOK TIME: 11 MIN | YIELDS 1 (6") PIE

Most people think of the hard candy when they think of butterscotch, but for this recipe the butterscotch flavor comes from the brown sugar used to flavor the custard. If you have some good scotch on hand, you can add a teaspoon at the end of simmering to flavor the custard.

INGREDIENTS

1 cup half-and-half

¼ cup packed light brown sugar

1 tablespoon cornstarch

1 large egg yolk

1 tablespoon unsalted butter

½ teaspoon pure vanilla extract, divided

1 Cookie Crust for One, baked and cooled (see recipe in this chapter)

¼ cup heavy whipping cream

1 tablespoon powdered sugar

1. In a medium saucepan, whisk together half-and-half, brown sugar, cornstarch, and egg yolk. Place pan over medium-low heat and whisk until mixture starts to steam, about 4 minutes. Whisk constantly until mixture thickens and starts to simmer, about 6 minutes. Cook 15 seconds, then remove from heat and stir in butter and ¼ teaspoon vanilla. Mix well.

2. Pour mixture into prepared Cookie Crust for One. Place a layer of plastic wrap directly on filling and chill 4 hours or overnight.

3. Once chilled, in a medium bowl, add cream, powdered sugar, and remaining ¼ teaspoon vanilla. Use a hand mixer to whip on medium speed until soft peaks form, about 2 minutes.

4. Spread cream over pie. Serve immediately or chill up to 1 hour.

PERSONAL SPINACH AND GRUYÈRE QUICHE

PREP TIME: 30 MIN | COOK TIME: 53 MIN | YIELDS 1 (6") QUICHE

Gruyère cheese is a Swiss-style cheese with a nutty flavor and creamy texture. It is often used for making fondue and has a pleasant earthy flavor when warm. If you are unable to find Gruyère cheese, you can use baby Swiss in its place.

INGREDIENTS

1 Personal-Sized Pastry Crust, unbaked (see recipe in this chapter)

2 teaspoons butter

1 cup baby spinach

2 large eggs

¼ cup whole milk

3 tablespoons heavy cream

⅛ teaspoon salt

⅛ teaspoon ground nutmeg

¼ cup shredded Gruyère cheese

1. Preheat oven to 350°F.

2. Roll out Personal-Sized Pastry Crust on a lightly floured surface until it forms an 8" circle. Slide dough into a 6" pie pan, making sure not to stretch or tug.

3. Line inside of crust with baking parchment or aluminum foil, fill with uncooked rice or dried beans, and bake 10 minutes. Remove weights and lining, prick bottom of crust four or five times with a fork, then return to oven another 3 minutes. Remove from oven and cool to room temperature.

4. In a medium skillet over medium heat, add butter. Once melted add spinach and cook, stirring often, until wilted, about 5 minutes. Remove from heat and transfer spinach to a colander. Press to release liquid. Transfer to a cutting board and finely chop. Set aside.

5. In a medium bowl, add eggs, milk, cream, salt, and nutmeg. Whisk until well combined.

6. Layer chopped spinach and cheese in bottom of par-baked pastry crust. Pour egg mixture over top.

7. Bake 35–40 minutes or until filling is golden brown and puffed all over. Cool 30 minutes before serving. Enjoy warm or at room temperature.

MINI APPLE BLUEBERRY COBBLER

PREP TIME: 30 MIN | COOK TIME: 30 MIN | YIELDS 1 (6") COBBLER

This cobbler is a celebration of fresh fruit and is wonderful on a warm summer day. Just a pinch of allspice in the topping and almond extract in the filling will add a little oomph to the flavors of the apples and blueberries.

INGREDIENTS

¼ cup all-purpose flour

¼ cup granulated sugar, divided

¼ teaspoon baking powder

⅛ teaspoon allspice

1 tablespoon cubed salted, butter, chilled

2 tablespoons whole milk

1 medium-sized firm baking apple, peeled, cored, and sliced

1 cup fresh blueberries

1 tablespoon cornstarch

¼ teaspoon pure vanilla extract

⅛ teaspoon almond extract

1. Preheat oven to 350°F and place a baking sheet on bottom rack of oven.

2. In a medium bowl, combine flour, 1 tablespoon sugar, baking powder, and allspice. Whisk well to combine. Add butter and use your fingers to rub mixture until it resembles coarse sand.

3. Make a well in dry ingredients and add milk. Gently stir until a shaggy batter forms and no dry flour remains. Set aside.

4. In a medium bowl, add apple, blueberries, 2 tablespoons sugar, cornstarch, vanilla, and almond extract. Toss well to coat. Transfer mixture to a 6" pie pan.

5. Dollop biscuit mixture evenly over fruit by heaping teaspoons. Sprinkle with remaining 1 tablespoon sugar.

6. Bake on heated baking sheet 30–35 minutes or until topping is golden brown and filling is bubbling.

7. Remove cobbler from oven and let cool 30 minutes before enjoying.

CHOCOLATE COBBLER

PREP TIME: 20 MIN | COOK TIME: 30 MIN | YIELDS 1 (7") COBBLER

Chocolate cobbler is a magical dish. You layer melted butter, a stiff cake batter, cocoa, sugar, and boiling water into a pan, and after baking, you end up with a cake-like top with a rich fudgy sauce underneath! Be sure to bake this on a foil-lined baking sheet, as the sauce can sometimes bubble over a little.

INGREDIENTS

1 tablespoon salted butter

½ cup granulated sugar, divided

4 teaspoons cocoa powder, divided

⅓ cup all-purpose flour

⅛ teaspoon baking powder

⅛ teaspoon baking soda

2 tablespoons whole milk

¼ teaspoon pure vanilla extract

⅓ cup boiling water

1. Preheat oven to 350°F.

2. Add butter to a 5" × 7" baking dish and place on a baking sheet lined with aluminum foil. Place in oven and bake until melted, about 5 minutes. Remove from oven and set aside.

3. In a medium bowl, add ¼ cup sugar, 2 teaspoons cocoa powder, flour, baking powder, and baking soda. Whisk to combine. Add milk and vanilla and stir to mix, then spread over melted butter. Add remaining ¼ cup sugar and remaining 2 teaspoons cocoa powder over top, then pour boiling water over it. Do not mix.

4. Bake 25–30 minutes or until top is set but the whole cobbler jiggles slightly when moved. Cool 20 minutes before serving.

CHAPTER 6

PUDDINGS AND CUSTARDS

When you think of elegant desserts, what comes to mind? Like many people, you probably think of things like a crème brûlée topped with a caramelized sugar crust, silky and rich chocolate pot de crème, and crisp chocolate éclairs stuffed with vanilla pastry cream. These desserts make you feel like you are having a special treat. If you have ever made any of these desserts at home, you know the recipes yield six, eight, or even twelve portions, and they do not keep all that well.

This chapter will help you to enjoy your favorite custard and pudding desserts in portions better suited to one person. From custard-filled Orange Cream Puffs and Chocolate Chip Croissant Bread Pudding to simple Flan for One and citrusy Crema Catalana, this chapter will offer you recipes as well as tips and tricks to make your single-serving desserts a success! While these recipes do take a little more time, they are absolutely worth it. The reward is the pleasure you will find while dipping your spoon into a perfectly baked custard, or sinking your teeth into a velvety bread pudding. Nothing is stopping you from indulging in an elegant dessert, and remember—you deserve it!

ORANGE CREAM PUFFS

PREP TIME: 20 MIN | COOK TIME: 39 MIN | YIELDS 4 (4") PUFFS

These crisp puffs have a bright orange flavor and are perfect when filled with traditional pastry cream, whipped cream, or even vanilla ice cream. If you choose ice cream, be sure to add a drizzle of chocolate over the top!

INGREDIENTS

3 tablespoons water

2 tablespoons orange juice

3 tablespoons salted butter

⅓ cup all-purpose flour

1 teaspoon granulated sugar

½ teaspoon freshly grated orange zest

1 large egg

¼ teaspoon pure vanilla extract

1 recipe Vanilla Pastry Cream (see recipe in this chapter)

2 tablespoons powdered sugar

1. Preheat oven to 400°F and line a baking sheet with parchment or a reusable silicone baking mat.

2. In a medium saucepan over medium heat, add water, orange juice, and butter. Bring mixture to a boil, then add flour, granulated sugar, and orange zest and cook, stirring constantly, until the mixture forms a smooth ball and a film develops on bottom of the pan, about 1 minute.

3. Remove pan from heat and transfer dough to a medium bowl. Let dough cool 10 minutes or until it is cool enough to touch.

4. Add egg and vanilla. Use a hand mixer on medium speed to beat until batter is smooth and glossy, about 30 seconds. Spoon dough onto the prepared baking sheet with two spoons into four mounds about 2" apart.

5. Bake 10 minutes, then reduce oven to 325°F and bake 25–30 minutes or until puffs are golden brown and puffed. Transfer to a rack and allow to cool to room temperature.

6. Once cool, slice each shell in half horizontally. Transfer Vanilla Pastry Cream into a piping bag fitted with a medium round tip. Pipe cream onto one half of each shell and top with second half.

7. Dust tops of puffs generously with powdered sugar before enjoying.

CHOCOLATE ÉCLAIRS

PREP TIME: 20 MIN | COOK TIME: 39 MIN | YIELDS 4 (4") ÉCLAIRS

A chocolate éclair is an elegant dessert that is easier to make than you think.

INGREDIENTS

⅓ cup water

3 tablespoons salted butter

⅓ cup all-purpose flour

1 teaspoon granulated sugar

1 large egg

¼ teaspoon pure vanilla extract

1 recipe Vanilla Pastry Cream (see recipe in this chapter)

2 tablespoons heavy whipping cream

¼ cup semisweet chocolate chips

1. Preheat oven to 400°F and line a baking sheet with parchment or a reusable silicone baking mat.

2. In a medium saucepan over medium heat, add water and butter. Bring to a boil, then add flour and sugar and cook, stirring constantly, until the mixture forms a smooth ball and a film develops on bottom of the pan, about 1 minute.

3. Remove pan from heat and transfer dough to a medium bowl. Let dough cool 10 minutes or until it is cool enough to touch.

4. Add egg and vanilla. Use a hand mixer on medium speed to beat until batter is smooth and glossy, about 30 seconds. Transfer mixture to a piping bag fitted with a large round (#9) tube. Pipe dough into six equal lines on baking sheet about 2" apart.

5. Bake 10 minutes, then reduce oven to 325°F and bake 25–30 minutes or until éclairs are golden brown and puffed. Transfer to a rack, gently poke a paring knife into the side of each éclair shell, and allow to cool to room temperature.

6. Once cool, slice each shell in half horizontally. Pipe Vanilla Pastry Cream into bottom of each shell.

7. In a small microwave-safe bowl, add cream and heat 30 seconds. Stir in chocolate chips and heat in 15-second intervals until chocolate is melted.

8. Dip top shell into chocolate, then place on top of filling. Refrigerate uncovered 10 minutes to set chocolate.

VANILLA PASTRY CREAM

PREP TIME: 4 HOURS | COOK TIME: 8 MIN | YIELDS 1 CUP

Pastry cream can be used to fill cakes and cupcakes, spread into a baked pastry crust and topped with fresh fruit, piped into cream puffs, or simply eaten with a spoon. If you want to make this cream even richer, use heavy cream in place of half-and-half. To make a chocolate version, add 1 teaspoon of cocoa powder.

INGREDIENTS

¾ cup half-and-half

3 tablespoons granulated sugar

1 tablespoon cornstarch

1 large egg yolk

¼ teaspoon pure vanilla extract

1 teaspoon unsalted butter

1. In a blender, combine half-and-half, sugar, corn-starch, and egg yolk. Purée until smooth, about 20 seconds.

2. Transfer mixture to a small saucepan and place over medium-low heat. Cook, whisking constantly, until mixture comes to a boil and thickens, about 8 minutes.

3. Remove from heat and whisk in vanilla and butter. Once smooth, pour mixture through a strainer into a medium bowl. Place a layer of plastic wrap directly on pastry cream and chill at least 4 hours before using.

BAKED EGG CUSTARD

PREP TIME: 4 HOURS | COOK TIME: 40 MIN | SERVES 1

Mace is the lacy coating outside of the nutmeg seed and is considered its sister spice. The flavor is very similar to nutmeg but lighter and blended with spicy cinnamon. If you do not have any mace, you can use nutmeg, preferably freshly grated, in its place.

INGREDIENTS

½ cup half-and-half

1 large egg yolk

1 tablespoon granulated sugar

⅛ teaspoon cornstarch

1 pinch (about 1/16 teaspoon) ground mace

1. Preheat oven to 325°F.

2. In a small bowl, combine half-and-half, egg yolk, sugar, and cornstarch. Whisk until smooth. Transfer mixture to a 7-ounce ramekin and dust top with mace.

3. Place ramekin in a small baking dish. Add recently boiled water until it reaches halfway up the side of the ramekin.

4. Bake 40–45 minutes or until custard is set around the edges but still a little jiggly in the center. Transfer ramekin to a wire rack and cool to room temperature, then chill at least 4 hours before enjoying.

Baked Custards

A baked custard, properly prepared, is silky and rich but not too heavy. You can't rush a baked custard, as it needs time to gently bake in a water bath and then needs some time to chill thoroughly. The water bath is key to gently cooking the custard, which will prevent it from curdling or splitting while baking, so don't skip that step.

CHOCOLATE CUSTARD

PREP TIME: 6 HOURS | COOK TIME: 38 MIN | SERVES 1

If you would like to make this into a Mexican hot chocolate–flavored treat, add ⅛ teaspoon cinnamon and a fat pinch of nutmeg to the sugar and cocoa powder, then proceed with the recipe as written.

INGREDIENTS

1 tablespoon granulated sugar

1 tablespoon cocoa powder

½ cup half-and-half

2 tablespoons semisweet chocolate chips

2 teaspoons unsalted butter

1 large egg yolk

¼ teaspoon pure vanilla extract

1. In a medium saucepan, add sugar and cocoa powder and whisk until well combined. Slowly whisk in half-and-half and heat over medium heat until sugar has melted and the mixture comes to a simmer, about 3 minutes. Remove from heat and whisk in chocolate chips and butter until smooth.

2. In a small bowl, whisk together egg yolk and vanilla. While whisking, ladle a few tablespoons of hot half-and-half mixture into the egg yolk, then whisk egg yolk mixture into half-and-half in pan.

3. Transfer mixture to a 7-ounce ramekin and chill 2 hours.

4. Preheat oven to 325°F.

5. Once chilled, place ramekin in a small baking dish. Add recently boiled water until it reaches halfway up the side of the ramekin.

6. Bake 35–40 minutes or until custard is set around edges but slightly jiggly in center. Transfer ramekin to a wire rack and cool to room temperature, then chill at least 4 hours before enjoying.

Custard Baking Tips

Baked custards should always be baked in a water bath unless otherwise noted. That gentle baking keeps the texture smooth. Watch the time carefully. Check early and test your custard by shaking the pan gently. Once ready, the edges should be set and the center should jiggle slightly. If you pull it too soon the custard will not set or it will be watery. If it overbakes, it will become grainy, similar to scrambled eggs.

PERSONAL BANANA PUDDING

PREP TIME: 20 MIN | COOK TIME: 13 MIN | SERVES 1

This version of banana pudding has a toasted meringue topping that is popular in the American South. It is generally served slightly warm, but if you wish to enjoy it chilled, simply cool to room temperature before refrigerating uncovered at least 2 hours.

INGREDIENTS

3 tablespoons plus 1 teaspoon granulated sugar, divided

1 tablespoon all-purpose flour

¾ cup half-and-half

1 large egg, yolk and white separated

¼ teaspoon pure vanilla extract

1 teaspoon salted butter

½ medium-sized ripe banana, peeled and sliced

6 vanilla wafer cookies

1 pinch (about 1⁄16 teaspoon) cream of tartar

1. Preheat oven to 400°F.

2. In a small saucepan, combine 3 tablespoons sugar and flour. Whisk to combine, then add half-and-half and egg yolk. Whisk until smooth.

3. Heat mixture over medium-low heat, whisking constantly, until it just comes to a boil and thickens, about 5 minutes. Remove pan from heat and whisk in vanilla and butter.

4. Spread ⅓ of custard mixture in bottom of a 7-ounce ramekin. Top with half of banana slices and 3 vanilla wafers. Repeat with remaining custard, bananas, and wafers, ending with a layer of custard.

5. In a medium bowl, add egg white and cream of tartar. Use a hand mixer on medium-low speed to beat egg white until foamy, then gradually add remaining 1 teaspoon sugar and continue to beat on high speed until stiff peaks form.

6. Spoon meringue over top of pudding, making sure meringue covers edges of ramekin. Bake 8–10 minutes or until meringue is golden brown. Remove from oven and cool 20 minutes before serving.

FLAN FOR ONE

If you do not want to make the caramel for the top of the flan you can use 1 tablespoon of prepared caramel sauce in its place. A good-quality caramel ice cream topping will work just as well as the homemade caramel, but the added cream gives it a creamier flavor.

INGREDIENTS

¼ cup granulated sugar, divided

1 teaspoon water

½ cup half-and-half

1 large egg yolk

¼ teaspoon pure vanilla extract

⅛ teaspoon cornstarch

1 pinch (about ¹⁄₁₆ teaspoon) ground cinnamon

1. Preheat oven to 325°F.

2. In a small saucepan, add 2 tablespoons sugar and water. Heat over medium heat until sugar melts and starts to turn golden brown, about 5 minutes. Immediately pour caramel into a 7-ounce ramekin and swirl so it covers bottom completely. Set aside.

3. In a small bowl, combine remaining 2 tablespoons sugar, half-and-half, egg yolk, vanilla, and cornstarch. Whisk until smooth, then add cinnamon and whisk until fully incorporated. Transfer mixture to ramekin.

4. Place ramekin in a small baking dish. Add recently boiled water until it reaches halfway up the side of the ramekin.

5. Bake 40–45 minutes or until custard is set around the edges but still a little jiggly in the center. Transfer ramekin to a wire rack and cool to room temperature. Run a thin knife around the edge of the custard to loosen, then place a small plate on ramekin and turn over until flan releases. Enjoy at room temperature or chilled.

RICE PUDDING

PREP TIME: 10 MIN | COOK TIME: 35 MIN | SERVES 1

Rice pudding is an excellent way to use leftover rice. This recipe calls for white rice, but you can use brown rice if that is what you have on hand. Feel free to use any dried fruits you like if raisins are not to your taste. Dried cranberries are lovely in this pudding!

INGREDIENTS

1 large egg

2 tablespoons whole milk

2 tablespoons granulated sugar

¼ teaspoon pure vanilla extract

⅛ teaspoon ground cinnamon

½ cup cooked white rice

2 tablespoons raisins

1. Preheat oven to 350°F and lightly spray a 7-ounce ramekin with nonstick cooking spray.

2. In a medium bowl, combine egg and milk. Whisk until fully incorporated, then add sugar, vanilla, and cinnamon and whisk well.

3. Add rice and raisins and stir to combine, then transfer to prepared ramekin. Place ramekin in a small baking dish. Add recently boiled water until it reaches halfway up the side of the ramekin.

4. Bake 35–40 minutes or until custard is set around the edges but still a little jiggly in the center. Transfer ramekin to a wire rack and cool 15 minutes before serving. Enjoy warm or at room temperature.

Making Small Batches of Rice
Making a single portion of rice can be tricky if you're using the traditional methods. An easier, if unconventional, way to get perfect rice in small portions is to boil it like pasta. Use three times the water to uncooked white rice, boil for 11 minutes, drain, then return to the pot. Cover and let stand 5 minutes. The rice will be fluffy and ready to enjoy.

ORANGE CRANBERRY BREAD PUDDING

PREP TIME: 30 MIN | COOK TIME: 30 MIN | SERVES 1

Rubbing the orange zest and sugar together helps to release more of the orange oil in the zest, which will infuse more of the custard with citrus flavor. If you want to add an extra special touch you can garnish the hot bread pudding with a tablespoon of white chocolate chips.

INGREDIENTS

1½ cups cubed bread, left out for 3 hours to dry out slightly

2 tablespoons dried cranberries

3 tablespoons granulated sugar

½ teaspoon freshly grated orange zest

1 large egg yolk

½ cup whole milk

¼ teaspoon pure vanilla extract

¼ teaspoon ground cinnamon

1 tablespoon unsalted butter, at room temperature

1. Preheat oven to 350°F and spray a 6" pie pan with nonstick cooking spray.

2. In a medium bowl, combine bread cubes and cranberries. Set aside.

3. In a small bowl, add sugar and orange zest. With your fingers, rub sugar and zest together until very fragrant. Whisk in egg yolk until smooth, then add milk, vanilla, and cinnamon and whisk until smooth.

4. Pour milk mixture over bread cubes and mix to combine. Let stand 10 minutes, stir again, then allow to stand 10 minutes more.

5. Transfer soaked bread and custard to prepared pan. Dot top with butter. Bake 30–35 minutes or until pudding is puffed all over and golden brown. Remove from oven and transfer to wire rack. Cool 15 minutes before serving. Enjoy warm.

CLASSIC BREAD PUDDING

PREP TIME: 30 MIN | COOK TIME: 30 MIN | SERVES 1

This bread pudding is simple to prepare and is satisfying but not too rich. If you would like to enjoy this for breakfast, you can prepare it the evening before, cover, and refrigerate overnight. The next morning, uncover and bake it straight from the refrigerator, adding 1 extra minute to the cooking time.

INGREDIENTS

1½ cups cubed bread, left out 3 hours to dry out slightly

2 tablespoons raisins

3 tablespoons packed light brown sugar

1 large egg yolk

½ cup whole milk

¼ teaspoon pure vanilla extract

¼ teaspoon ground cinnamon

1 tablespoon unsalted butter, at room temperature

1. Preheat oven to 350°F and spray a 6¼" cast iron skillet with nonstick cooking spray.

2. In a medium bowl, add bread cubes and raisins. Set aside.

3. In a small bowl, whisk together brown sugar and egg yolk. Add milk, vanilla, and cinnamon and whisk until smooth.

4. Pour milk mixture over bread cubes and mix to combine. Let stand 10 minutes, stir again, then allow to stand more 10 minutes.

5. Transfer soaked bread and custard to prepared skillet. Dot top with butter. Bake 30–35 minutes or until pudding is puffed all over and golden brown. Remove from oven and transfer to wire rack. Cool 15 minutes before serving. Enjoy warm.

Bread for Bread Pudding

Most crusty or sandwich bread works well for bread pudding. It is an excellent way to use up heels and stale slices that no one wants. You can stash leftover pieces of bread in an airtight container in the freezer to use for bread pudding later. Cube it up before freezing, then thaw it 1 hour before proceeding with your recipe.

CRÈME BRÛLÉE

PREP TIME: 2½ HOURS | COOK TIME: 23 MIN | SERVES 1

Perhaps one of the most elegant desserts out there, crème brûlée is exceptionally creamy and rich with a crisp candy sugar topping. If you do not have a kitchen torch, heat your broiler, place a rack near the top of the oven, and broil the sugar until it melts. It only takes a few minutes, so keep an eye on it to prevent scorching.

INGREDIENTS

½ cup heavy cream

¼ teaspoon vanilla bean paste

2 large egg yolks

¼ cup granulated sugar, divided

1. Preheat oven to 300°F.

2. In a small saucepan, add cream and vanilla bean paste. Heat over medium heat until cream simmers, about 3 minutes. Set aside.

3. In a small bowl, combine egg yolks and 3 table-spoons sugar. Whisk until smooth, then slowly whisk in hot cream. Transfer mixture to a 7-ounce ramekin.

4. Place ramekin in a small baking dish. Add recently boiled water until it reaches halfway up the side of the ramekin.

5. Bake 20–25 minutes or until custard is set around the edges but still a little jiggly in the center. Transfer ramekin to a wire rack and cool to room temperature, then chill at least 2 hours.

6. To serve, sprinkle remaining 1 tablespoon sugar evenly over top of custard. With a small torch, or under a heated broiler, melt sugar until caramelized. Cool 2 minutes to allow sugar to harden before enjoying.

SPICED CARDAMOM CUSTARD

PREP TIME: 4½ HOURS | COOK TIME: 40 MIN | SERVES 1

Cardamom is a member of the ginger family and is a pod containing many fragrant seeds. It is popular in Indian cuisine, features prominently in chai tea, and pairs well with cinnamon and chocolate.

INGREDIENTS

½ cup half-and-half

1 large egg yolk

1 tablespoon packed dark brown sugar

½ teaspoon freshly grated orange zest

⅛ teaspoon ground cardamom

⅛ teaspoon ground cinnamon

⅛ teaspoon pure vanilla extract

1. Preheat oven to 325°F.

2. In a small bowl, combine half-and-half, egg yolk, and brown sugar. Whisk until smooth, then add orange zest, cardamom, cinnamon, and vanilla and whisk until fully incorporated. Transfer mixture to a 7-ounce ramekin.

3. Place ramekin in a small baking dish. Add recently boiled water until it reaches halfway up the side of the ramekin.

4. Bake 40–45 minutes or until custard is set around the edges but still a little jiggly in the center. Transfer ramekin to a wire rack and cool to room temperature, then chill at least 4 hours before enjoying.

CHOCOLATE CHIP CROISSANT BREAD PUDDING

PREP TIME: 30 MIN | COOK TIME: 30 MIN | SERVES 1

If you are looking for an extra-buttery dessert studded with chocolate, then you have hit the jackpot with this recipe! Croissants make for an extra-decadent bread pudding, due to the butter used to puff the layers. If you are using fresh croissants you will want to let the cubes stand uncovered for at least a few hours to dry out so the custard absorbs better.

INGREDIENTS

1½ cups cubed stale croissants

3 tablespoons semisweet chocolate chips, divided

3 tablespoons granulated sugar

1 large egg yolk

½ cup half-and-half

1 teaspoon bourbon

¼ teaspoon pure vanilla extract

1 tablespoon unsalted butter, at room temperature

1. Preheat oven to 350°F and spray a 6" pie pan with nonstick cooking spray.

2. In a medium bowl, add croissant cubes and 2 tablespoons chocolate chips. Set aside.

3. In a small bowl whisk, together sugar and egg yolk until smooth. Add half-and-half, bourbon, and vanilla and whisk until smooth.

4. Pour custard mixture over bread cubes and mix to combine. Let stand 10 minutes, stir again, then allow to stand 10 minutes more.

5. Transfer soaked bread and custard to prepared pan. Dot top with butter. Bake 30–35 minutes or until pudding is puffed all over and golden brown. Remove from oven, transfer to wire rack, and garnish with remaining 1 tablespoon chocolate chips. Cool 15 minutes before serving. Enjoy warm.

Why Stale Bread?

Stale bread is generally used for things like bread pudding and French toast because it absorbs liquids better. Fresh bread will result in an uneven texture since the custard will not fully absorb into it. You can use your oven to speed up the process. Place your bread on a baking sheet and bake at 225°F until dry and crusty, about 30 minutes.

MICROWAVE BREAD PUDDING

PREP TIME: 10 MIN | COOK TIME: 3 MIN | SERVES 1

What happens when you are short on time but really need some bread pudding? You turn to the microwave! This version is ready in a flash and will satisfy any bread pudding craving. Enjoy this warm because it is somewhat less charming when eaten cold.

INGREDIENTS

1 cup cubed sandwich bread

1 tablespoon golden raisins

1 large egg

¼ cup half-and-half

2 tablespoons whole milk

2 tablespoons granulated sugar

¼ teaspoon pure vanilla extract

⅛ teaspoon ground nutmeg

1 teaspoon powdered sugar

1. In a microwave-safe 10-ounce dish, place bread and raisins.

2. In a small bowl, combine egg, half-and-half, milk, granulated sugar, and vanilla. Whisk well, then pour mixture over bread. Sprinkle top with nutmeg.

3. Microwave 1 minute, then check to see if there is any liquid remaining in dish. Continue to microwave in 30-second intervals until no liquid remains.

4. Remove from microwave and cool 2 minutes. Dust with powdered sugar and enjoy warm.

CREMA CATALANA

PREP TIME: 4½ HOURS | COOK TIME: 6 MIN | SERVES 1

This Spanish custard is similar to crème brûlée with a caramelized sugar topping and creamy custard, but where crème brûlée is slowly baked in a water bath, Crema Catalana is cooked entirely on the stove. It is flavored with orange, lemon, and cinnamon, popular flavors in Spain, which is known for growing citrus.

INGREDIENTS

½ cup plus 1 tablespoon whole milk

2 tablespoons granulated sugar, divided

1½ teaspoons cornstarch

1" strip fresh orange zest

1" strip fresh lemon zest

½ cinnamon stick

1 large egg yolk, beaten

¼ teaspoon pure vanilla extract

1. In a small saucepan, add milk, 1 tablespoon plus 2 teaspoons sugar, and cornstarch. Whisk until smooth, then add orange zest, lemon zest, and cinnamon stick. Heat over medium-low heat and cook, whisking constantly, until mixture comes to a simmer, about 3 minutes.

2. In a small bowl, add egg yolk and vanilla. Whisk 3 tablespoons of hot milk mixture into egg yolk, then whisk yolk mixture back into milk in pan. Continue to cook until custard is bubbling and thick, about 3 minutes.

3. Strain custard into a 7-ounce ramekin and smooth top. Place a layer of plastic wrap directly on custard, then refrigerate 4 hours or until fully chilled.

4. To serve, sprinkle top with remaining 1 teaspoon sugar. With a small torch, or under a heated broiler, melt sugar until caramelized. Cool 2 minutes to allow sugar to harden before enjoying.

How to Make Citrus Zest Strips

To make strips of fresh citrus zest you only need a vegetable peeler. Take your citrus and pull the vegetable peeler down the fruit to slice off a strip of zest. Do not press too hard, or you will get too much of the pith, which can make your mixture bitter. Be sure to cover the citrus with plastic wrap and refrigerate so the fruit does not dry out before you can eat it.

BREAD AND BUTTER PUDDING

PREP TIME: 1½ HOURS | COOK TIME: 32 MIN | SERVES 1

Bread and butter pudding is popular in British cuisine. You can use standard sandwich bread, or, if you have brioche or challah in your bread box you can use either one to add extra richness. The amaretto can be omitted if you do not have it on hand.

INGREDIENTS

3 tablespoons boiling water

2 tablespoons golden raisins

1 teaspoon amaretto

2 tablespoons unsalted butter, at room temperature

3 slices white bread, crusts removed

2 large egg yolks

3 tablespoons plus 1 teaspoon granulated sugar, divided

6 tablespoons heavy cream

2 tablespoons half-and-half

¼ teaspoon vanilla bean paste

1. In a small bowl, add water and raisins. Let stand 1 hour, then drain and add amaretto. Set aside.

2. Preheat oven to 350°F and spray a 6" pie pan with nonstick cooking spray.

3. Butter bread slices on both sides. Cut 1 slice into ½" cubes. Cut remaining slices into four triangles. Set aside.

4. In a small bowl, whisk together egg yolks and 3 tablespoons sugar until smooth. Set aside.

5. In a small saucepan, add cream and half-and-half. Heat over medium heat until milk just comes to a simmer, about 2 minutes. Add 2 tablespoons hot cream mixture to egg yolks and whisk well, then whisk mixture back into saucepan. Immediately remove from heat and stir in vanilla bean paste.

6. Lay cubed bread on base of prepared pie pan. Top with raisins, then place bread triangles over top. Pour custard over bread, making sure each slice is evenly coated. Let stand 10 minutes at room temperature to soak.

7. Place pie pan in a larger baking dish and add recently boiled water until it reaches halfway up the pan. Bake 30 minutes or until filling is set. Remove from oven and transfer to wire rack.

8. Sprinkle remaining 1 teaspoon sugar over top and torch or broil until sugar is caramelized. Serve warm or at room temperature.

PAN DE CALATRAVA

PREP TIME: 2½ HOURS | COOK TIME: 38 MIN | SERVES 1

This recipe is a variation of a Spanish custard bread pudding. The texture is thick and creamy, but not too heavy because of the French bread. There is also a hint of citrus, which adds a refreshing taste. This pudding can be made with stale cake cubes, crusty bread cubes, or even leftover hard cookies like biscotti.

INGREDIENTS

½ cup cubed French bread, left out 4 hours to dry out slightly

½ cup plus 2 tablespoons whole milk

3 tablespoons granulated sugar

1" strip fresh lemon zest

1 large egg yolk

¼ teaspoon pure vanilla extract

1 pinch (about ⅟₁₆ teaspoon) ground cinnamon

1. Preheat oven to 325°F.

2. Lightly spray an 8-ounce ramekin with nonstick cooking spray. Arrange bread cubes in ramekin. Set aside.

3. In a small saucepan, add milk, sugar, and lemon zest. Heat over medium-low heat and cook, whisking constantly, until mixture comes to a simmer, about 3 minutes.

4. In a small bowl, add egg yolk and vanilla. Whisk 3 tablespoons of hot milk mixture into egg yolk, then whisk yolk mixture back into milk in pan. Remove pan from heat and strain mixture into prepared ramekin. Sprinkle cinnamon over top.

5. Place ramekin in a small baking dish. Add recently boiled water until it reaches halfway up the side of the ramekin.

6. Bake 35–40 minutes or until custard is set around the edges but still a little jiggly in the center. Transfer ramekin to a wire rack and cool to room temperature, then chill 2 hours.

7. To serve, run a thin knife around the edge of the custard to loosen, then place a small plate on ramekin and turn over until custard releases. Enjoy at room temperature or chilled.

BUTTERSCOTCH CUSTARD

PREP TIME: 6½ HOURS | COOK TIME: 38 MIN | SERVES 1

Butterscotch is similar to caramel, but it has a richer flavor because it starts with brown sugar rather than white sugar. It is thought to have originated in Yorkshire in the nineteenth century. Butterscotch can be made into a sauce for pouring over cakes and ice cream, or it can be whisked into custards like the one you find here!

INGREDIENTS

3 tablespoons packed dark brown sugar

2 teaspoons unsalted butter

½ cup half-and-half

1 large egg yolk

¼ teaspoon pure vanilla extract

⅛ teaspoon cornstarch

1. In a medium saucepan, add brown sugar and butter. Heat over medium heat until sugar has melted. Whisk in half-and-half until smooth, then allow mixture to come to a simmer, about 3 minutes. Remove from heat.

2. In a small bowl, whisk together egg yolk, vanilla, and cornstarch. While whisking, ladle a few tablespoons of hot half-and-half mixture into the egg yolk, then whisk egg yolk mixture into half-and-half in the pan.

3. Transfer mixture to a 7-ounce ramekin and chill 2 hours.

4. Preheat oven to 325°F.

5. Once chilled, cover ramekin with aluminum foil, poke a few holes into foil to release steam, and place ramekin in a small baking dish. Add recently boiled water until it reaches halfway up the side of the ramekin.

6. Bake 35–40 minutes or until custard is set around edges but slightly jiggly in center. Transfer ramekin to a wire rack and cool to room temperature, then chill at least 4 hours before enjoying.

BAKED COFFEE CUSTARD

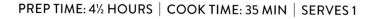

PREP TIME: 4½ HOURS | COOK TIME: 35 MIN | SERVES 1

This custard is the dessert form of a coffee shop classic—iced vanilla latte. Instant espresso powder can be found in the coffee aisle along with instant coffee, and it offers the richest flavor here. If you do not use espresso powder often, you can store it in your freezer up to a year.

INGREDIENTS

½ cup half-and-half

1 large egg yolk

1 tablespoon granulated sugar

¼ teaspoon instant espresso powder

¼ teaspoon cocoa powder

⅛ teaspoon pure vanilla extract

1. Preheat oven to 325°F.

2. In a small bowl, combine half-and-half, egg yolk, sugar, espresso powder, cocoa powder, and vanilla. Whisk until smooth. Transfer mixture to a 7-ounce ramekin.

3. Place ramekin in a small baking dish. Add recently boiled water until it reaches halfway up the side of the ramekin.

4. Bake 35–40 minutes or until custard is set around the edges but still a little jiggly in the center. Transfer ramekin to a wire rack and cool to room temperature, then chill at least 4 hours before enjoying.

EGGNOG CUSTARD

PREP TIME: 4½ HOURS | COOK TIME: 35 MIN | SERVES 1

Around the holiday season eggnog is a popular treat, often spiked with a little whiskey or rum. Here the delicious flavors of eggnog are baked into an ultra-rich custard dessert. The whiskey called for is totally optional. It can be replaced with spiced rum or ⅛ teaspoon rum extract if desired.

INGREDIENTS

¼ cup half-and-half

¼ cup heavy cream

1 large egg yolk

1 tablespoon granulated sugar

1 teaspoon whiskey

¼ teaspoon pure vanilla extract

⅛ teaspoon ground cinnamon

1 pinch (about ¹⁄₁₆ teaspoon) ground nutmeg

1. Preheat oven to 325°F.

2. In a small bowl, combine half-and-half, cream, egg yolk, sugar, whiskey, vanilla, cinnamon, and nutmeg. Whisk until smooth. Transfer mixture to a 7-ounce ramekin.

3. Place ramekin in a small baking dish. Add recently boiled water until it reaches halfway up the side of the ramekin.

4. Bake 35–40 minutes or until custard is set around the edges but still a little jiggly in the center. Transfer ramekin to a wire rack and cool to room temperature, then chill at least 4 hours before enjoying.

CINNAMON DULCE DE LECHE FLAN

PREP TIME: 10 MIN | COOK TIME: 45 MIN | SERVES 1

Dulce de leche can be purchased in a resealable squeeze bottle in most well-stocked grocery stores either in the ice cream toppings aisle or with Latin American foods. It is a caramelized condensed milk and is often used in coffee and desserts. It keeps for months in the refrigerator.

INGREDIENTS

3 tablespoons granulated sugar, divided

1 teaspoon water

¼ cup half-and-half

¼ cup dulce de leche

1 large egg yolk

¼ teaspoon pure vanilla extract

⅛ teaspoon cornstarch

⅛ teaspoon ground cinnamon

1. Preheat oven to 325°F.

2. In a small saucepan, add 2 tablespoons sugar and water. Heat over medium heat until sugar melts and starts to turn golden brown, about 5 minutes. Immediately pour resulting caramel into a 7-ounce ramekin and swirl so it covers bottom completely. Set aside.

3. In a small bowl, combine remaining 1 tablespoon sugar, half-and-half, dulce de leche, egg yolk, vanilla, and cornstarch. Whisk until smooth, then add cinnamon and whisk until fully incorporated. Transfer mixture to ramekin.

4. Place ramekin in a small baking dish. Add recently boiled water until it reaches halfway up the side of the ramekin.

5. Bake 40–45 minutes or until custard is set around the edges but still a little jiggly in the center. Transfer ramekin to a wire rack and cool to room temperature. Run a thin knife around the edge of the custard to loosen, then place a small plate on ramekin and turn over until flan releases. Enjoy at room temperature or chilled.

RASPBERRY CUSTARD CAKE

PREP TIME: 10 MIN | COOK TIME: 30 MIN | SERVES 1

This dish is a personal-sized take on raspberry custard kuchen, a popular German dessert. It is a hybrid of cake and custard studded with tangy raspberries. This is best when made with fresh berries, so if raspberries are not available feel free to use fresh blackberries, blueberries, cherries, or diced strawberries.

INGREDIENTS

2 tablespoons all-purpose flour, divided

1½ teaspoons cubed salted butter

1 tablespoon plus ½ teaspoon heavy cream, divided

1 tablespoon plus ½ teaspoon granulated sugar, divided

¼ cup fresh raspberries

1 large egg yolk

¼ teaspoon cornstarch

¼ teaspoon pure vanilla extract

1. Preheat oven to 350°F and lightly spray a 7-ounce ramekin with nonstick cooking spray. Set aside.

2. In a small bowl, combine 1 tablespoon plus 2 teaspoons all-purpose flour and butter. Use your fingers to rub butter into flour until well combined. Add ½ teaspoon cream and mix to combine.

3. Press dough into prepared ramekin and sprinkle remaining 1 teaspoon flour and ½ teaspoon sugar on top, then arrange raspberries over top. Set aside.

4. In a small bowl, whisk together remaining 1 tablespoon sugar, remaining 1 tablespoon cream, egg yolk, cornstarch, and vanilla. Pour over raspberries.

5. Bake 30–35 minutes or until custard is puffed and just golden brown around the edges. Cool to room temperature before enjoying.

Is the Custard Really Done?

If you are new to custard making you may want to double-check your shake test with another method until you become more confident. You can use a thin paring knife dipped in just off center of the custard. If it comes out clean, then your custard is ready. If it has any custard clinging to the blade, add another few minutes to the cooking time.

CHOCOLATE POT DE CRÈME

PREP TIME: 4½ HOURS | COOK TIME: 53 MIN | SERVES 1

This French dessert is originally from the seventeenth century and is called *pot de crème*, meaning "pot of custard." It is subtly sweet and richly chocolatey, and is the perfect treat for people who love a more sophisticated chocolate dessert. Use the best-quality chocolate you can find because the chocolate is really the star flavor.

INGREDIENTS

⅓ cup heavy cream

2 tablespoons whole milk

1 ounce finely chopped bittersweet chocolate

1 large egg yolk

2 teaspoons granulated sugar

⅛ teaspoon pure vanilla extract

1. Preheat oven to 325°F.

2. In a small saucepan over medium heat, heat cream and milk to a bare simmer, about 3 minutes. Remove from heat and add chocolate. Whisk until smooth, then add egg yolk, sugar, and vanilla. Whisk until smooth.

3. Pour mixture into a 7-ounce ramekin and cover tightly with aluminum foil. Place ramekin into a small baking dish. Add recently boiled water until it reaches halfway up the side of the ramekin.

4. Bake 50–55 minutes or until custard is set around the edges but still a little jiggly in the center. Transfer ramekin to a wire rack and cool to room temperature, then chill at least 4 hours before enjoying.

BAKED CHOCOLATE PUDDING CAKE

PREP TIME: 15 MIN | COOK TIME: 33 MIN | SERVES 1

This baked dessert is similar to a flourless chocolate cake but is lighter in texture. When cooled to room temperature it is like a rich mousse, but you can chill it and enjoy it cold. When cold, the texture is more dense and fudgy. This recipe calls for the best-quality bittersweet chocolate—the darker the better!

INGREDIENTS

1½ tablespoons salted butter, at room temperature

2 ounces finely chopped bittersweet chocolate

1 large egg, yolk and white separated

1 pinch (about ⅟16 teaspoon) cream of tartar

2 tablespoons granulated sugar, divided

1. Preheat oven to 350°F.

2. In a small microwave-safe bowl, add butter and chocolate. Microwave 30 seconds, stir well, then microwave in 15-second intervals until fully melted. Set aside.

3. In a medium bowl, add egg white and cream of tartar. Use a hand mixer to beat egg white on medium speed until foamy, about 30 seconds, then gradually add 1 tablespoon sugar and beat on high speed until stiff peaks form, about 1 minute. Set aside.

4. In a small bowl, beat together egg yolk and remaining 1 tablespoon sugar until light in color, about 2 minutes. Add chocolate mixture to egg yolk mixture and mix to combine, about 20 seconds.

5. Fold half of egg white into chocolate mixture until just combined, then add remaining egg white and fold until no streaks remain.

6. Spoon batter into an 8-ounce ramekin. Bake 30–35 minutes or until puffed yet still jiggly in the center. Transfer to a wire rack to cool to room temperature before serving.

BAKED LEMON PUDDING

PREP TIME: 15 MIN | COOK TIME: 30 MIN | SERVES 1

Part silky pudding; part cake; and all warm, comforting deliciousness! The magic of this pudding happens while baking. It splits into two layers, forming a custardy pudding on the bottom and a rich, cake-like layer on the top. If you want more lemon flavor, feel free to add up to ½ teaspoon more lemon zest.

INGREDIENTS

1 large egg, yolk and white separated

1 pinch (about ¹⁄₁₆ teaspoon) cream of tartar

2 tablespoons granulated sugar, divided

1½ tablespoons salted butter, at room temperature

2 teaspoons lemon juice

½ teaspoon freshly grated lemon zest

2 teaspoons all-purpose flour

2 tablespoons whole milk

1. Preheat oven to 350°F.

2. In a medium bowl, add egg white and cream of tartar. Use a hand mixer to beat egg white on medium speed until foamy, about 20 seconds, then gradually add 1 tablespoon sugar and beat on high speed until stiff peaks form, about 1 minute. Set aside.

3. In a small bowl, beat together butter and remaining 1 tablespoon sugar until light in color, about 2 minutes. Add egg yolk, lemon juice, and lemon zest and beat 1 minute or until well combined and lighter in color.

4. Add flour and milk and mix on low speed until incorporated and smooth, about 15 seconds. Fold half of egg white into yolk mixture until just combined, then add remaining egg white and fold until no streaks remain.

5. Spoon batter into an 8-ounce ramekin. Place ramekin in a small baking dish. Add recently boiled water until it reaches halfway up the side of the ramekin.

6. Bake 30–35 minutes or until pudding is golden brown and set on the top. Transfer ramekin to a wire rack and cool 10 minutes before enjoying.

CREAM CHEESE CUSTARD

PREP TIME: 4½ HOURS | COOK TIME: 35 MIN | SERVES 1

Cream cheese adds a subtle tang to this extra-rich and creamy custard, and the brown sugar adds a delicate caramel sweetness. If you would like to make this more like flan de queso (cheese flan), add a tablespoon of caramel sauce to the bottom of the ramekin before adding the custard.

INGREDIENTS

1 ounce cream cheese, at room temperature

2 tablespoons packed light brown sugar

1 large egg yolk

⅓ cup half-and-half

¼ teaspoon pure vanilla extract

1. Preheat oven to 325°F.

2. In a medium bowl, add cream cheese and brown sugar. Use a hand mixer on medium speed to beat until smooth and creamy, about 30 seconds.

3. Add egg yolk and beat until completely incorporated, then slowly beat in half-and-half until smooth. Stir in vanilla.

4. Transfer mixture to a 7-ounce ramekin. Place ramekin in a small baking dish. Add recently boiled water until it reaches halfway up the side of the ramekin.

5. Bake 35–40 minutes or until custard is set around edges but slightly jiggly in center. Transfer ramekin to a wire rack and cool to room temperature, then chill at least 4 hours before enjoying.

QUICK MICROWAVE CUSTARD PUDDING

PREP TIME: 2¼ HOURS | COOK TIME: 8 MIN | SERVES 1

You might be surprised, but yes, you can make custard in the microwave! This microwave custard recipe does not require cooking on the stove or water baths, making it simple and quick to make. Drizzle the top of the custard with caramel sauce, or serve it with whipped cream and raspberries.

INGREDIENTS

¾ cup whole milk

1 large egg

1 tablespoon granulated sugar

⅛ teaspoon pure vanilla extract

1 pinch (about ¹⁄₁₆ teaspoon) ground cinnamon

1. In a small bowl, combine milk, egg, sugar, and vanilla. Whisk until smooth. Transfer mixture to a 10-ounce microwave-safe ramekin. Sprinkle cinnamon over top.

2. Microwave at 50 percent power 6 minutes, then check if custard is set. If not, continue to microwave in 30-second intervals until custard is set fully.

3. Remove from microwave and refrigerate 2 hours before serving. Enjoy cold.

CHOCOLATE PECAN BREAD PUDDING

PREP TIME: 30 MIN | COOK TIME: 30 MIN | SERVES 1

Brioche is a very rich bread made with more eggs and butter than most sweet bread recipes. Brioche rolls are usually available in the bakery section of most grocery stores, and they can be frozen up to three months, thawed, and eaten as is, or used in recipes like this one. Because this bread is so rich, it takes a little longer to go stale, so leave it out at least 6 hours.

INGREDIENTS

1½ cups cubed brioche bread, left out 6 hours to dry out slightly

2 tablespoons chopped pecans

⅓ cup semisweet chocolate chips, divided

3 tablespoons granulated sugar

1 large egg yolk

1½ teaspoons cocoa powder

½ cup whole milk

¼ teaspoon pure vanilla extract

1 tablespoon unsalted butter, at room temperature

1. Preheat oven to 350°F and spray a 6" pie pan with nonstick cooking spray.

2. In a medium bowl, add bread cubes, pecans, and ¼ cup chocolate chips. Set aside.

3. In a small bowl, add sugar, egg yolk, and cocoa powder and whisk until smooth, then add milk and vanilla. Whisk until smooth.

4. Pour milk mixture over bread cubes and mix to combine. Let stand 10 minutes, stir again, then allow to stand 10 minutes more.

5. Transfer soaked bread and custard to prepared pie pan. Dot top with butter. Bake 30–35 minutes or until pudding is puffed all over and golden brown. Remove from oven and transfer to wire rack. Top with remaining chocolate chips. Cool 15 minutes before serving. Enjoy warm.

CHAPTER 7

MUFFINS AND QUICK BREADS

Muffins and quick breads are incredibly versatile and easy to make. Need breakfast on the go? Muffins have you covered, often in less than 30 minutes from start to finish. Want a sweet snack with a cup of afternoon tea? A loaf or quick bread for one is there to help. Want a bread side for your dinner? A small batch of savory muffins has your back and can be made at a moment's notice. Taking just a few moments to prepare and often requiring nothing more than a bowl, spatula, and pan, muffins and quick breads are some of the easiest yet most satisfying baked goods going.

For muffins and quick breads freshness is key. You certainly can freeze leftover muffins and slices of quick bread, but they are always better fresh. This chapter is packed with small-batch muffin recipes and individual quick bread recipes that are mouthwatering, easy, and ready in a snap so you never have to worry about dry muffins or stale quick bread. You will find classics like Blueberry Muffins and Pumpkin Bread along with more savory options like Jalapeño Corn Muffins and Savory Cheddar Ale Muffins. So, from grab-and-go snacks to break-time treats, you always have time for fresh and fabulous treats made just for you!

BLUEBERRY MUFFINS

PREP TIME: 10 MIN | COOK TIME: 18 MIN | YIELDS 4 MUFFINS

Blueberry Muffins are an excellent way to use frozen blueberries, so you can enjoy these muffins any time of year, even when berries are not in season or not their most flavorful. If you like you can use any sort of berry here, but if you use raspberries or blackberries, select fresh instead of frozen, as the frozen berries can be watery.

INGREDIENTS

½ cup all-purpose flour, divided

¼ cup blueberries

¼ cup granulated sugar

¼ teaspoon baking powder

⅛ teaspoon ground cinnamon

⅛ teaspoon baking soda

⅛ teaspoon salt

¼ cup whole milk

1 large egg, at room temperature

1 tablespoon unsalted butter, melted and cooled

¼ teaspoon pure vanilla extract

⅛ teaspoon almond extract

1. Preheat oven to 350°F and line four cups of a muffin pan with paper liners.

2. In a small bowl, add 1 teaspoon flour and blueberries. Gently toss until berries are coated in flour. Set aside.

3. In a medium bowl, add remaining flour, sugar, baking powder, cinnamon, baking soda, and salt. Whisk to combine. Set aside.

4. In a small bowl, combine milk, egg, butter, vanilla, and almond extract and whisk to combine. Pour wet ingredients into dry ingredients and use a spatula to mix until just combined, about six strokes, then add blueberries and fold to combine, four to six strokes. Do not overmix.

5. Divide batter between prepared muffin cups. Bake 18–20 minutes or until muffins spring back when gently pressed in the center and tops are golden brown. Cool in pan 3 minutes, then transfer to a wire rack to cool to room temperature.

Mix-In Ingredients

If your mixed-in ingredients like berries, chips, or nuts tend to sink, there is a quick trick that will help keep them suspended in the batter. Simply add 1 teaspoon flour to your mix-ins and toss until evenly coated. The flour will help suspend the mix-ins in the batter while they bake and keep them from sinking to the bottom.

CHOCOLATE BANANA BREAD

PREP TIME: 10 MIN | COOK TIME: 30 MIN | SERVES 1

Bananas with mostly black skins are perfect for making banana bread. They have the most potent banana flavor. If you keep bananas in the freezer for making smoothies and shakes, you can use them for banana bread too. Let the banana thaw in the refrigerator until soft enough to mash, then use it as directed in the recipe.

INGREDIENTS

⅓ cup all-purpose flour

¼ cup packed light brown sugar

1 tablespoon Dutch-processed cocoa powder

¼ teaspoon baking powder

¼ teaspoon ground cinnamon

⅛ teaspoon baking soda

⅛ teaspoon salt

¼ cup mashed very ripe banana (about ½ medium banana)

2 tablespoons buttermilk

1 large egg, at room temperature

1 tablespoon unsalted butter, melted and cooled

¼ teaspoon pure vanilla extract

2 tablespoons semisweet chocolate chips

3 tablespoons chopped walnuts, divided

1. Preheat oven to 350°F and spray a 5" × 3" mini-loaf pan with nonstick cooking spray.

2. In a medium bowl, add flour, brown sugar, cocoa powder, baking powder, cinnamon, baking soda, and salt. Whisk to combine. Set aside.

3. In a small bowl, combine banana, buttermilk, egg, butter, and vanilla. Whisk to combine. Pour wet ingredients into dry ingredients and use a spatula to mix until just combined, about six strokes, then add chocolate chips and 2 tablespoons walnuts and fold to combine, four to six strokes. Do not overmix.

4. Transfer batter to prepared pan and top with remaining 1 tablespoon walnuts. Bake 30–35 minutes or until bread springs back when gently pressed in the center and top is golden brown. Cool in pan 3 minutes, then transfer to a wire rack to cool to room temperature.

CHOCOLATE CHIP MUFFINS

PREP TIME: 10 MIN | COOK TIME: 18 MIN | YIELDS 4 MUFFINS

These muffins have a flavor that is reminiscent of chocolate chip cookies, so if you enjoy chocolate chip cookies then you will love these. If you want the chocolate to be more evenly spread throughout the muffins, you can swap the regular-sized chips for miniature chips. You can also use milk, white, or even butterscotch chips if you like.

INGREDIENTS

½ cup plus 2 tablespoons all-purpose flour, divided

2 tablespoons granulated sugar

1 tablespoon cubed unsalted butter, chilled

⅓ cup semisweet chocolate chips

¼ cup packed light brown sugar

¼ teaspoon baking powder

⅛ teaspoon baking soda

⅛ teaspoon salt

¼ cup whole milk

1 large egg, at room temperature

1 tablespoon unsalted butter, melted and cooled

¼ teaspoon pure vanilla extract

1. Preheat oven to 350°F and line four cups of a muffin pan with paper liners.

2. In a small bowl, combine 2 tablespoons flour, granulated sugar, and chilled butter. Use your fingers to mix until mixture clumps together and is crumbly. Chill until ready to use.

3. In a second small bowl, add 1 teaspoon flour and chocolate chips. Gently toss until chips are coated in flour. Set aside.

4. In a medium bowl, add remaining flour, brown sugar, baking powder, baking soda, and salt. Whisk to combine. Set aside.

5. In a third small bowl, combine milk, egg, melted butter, and vanilla and whisk to combine. Pour wet ingredients into dry ingredients and use a spatula to mix until just combined, about six strokes, then add chocolate chips and fold to combine, four to six strokes. Do not overmix.

6. Divide batter between prepared muffin cups. Sprinkle chilled topping evenly over muffins. Bake 18–20 minutes or until muffins spring back when gently pressed in the center and tops are golden brown. Cool in pan 3 minutes, then transfer to a wire rack to cool to room temperature.

CORN BREAD HONEY MUFFINS

PREP TIME: 10 MIN | COOK TIME: 18 MIN | YIELDS 4 MUFFINS

These lightly sweet Corn Bread Honey Muffins are perfect served with savory meals like spicy chili, smoked meats, or fried chicken. If you would like a little kick of spice, feel free to add a couple of fat pinches of cayenne pepper along with the dry ingredients. It will add a little tingle of heat with each bite.

INGREDIENTS

¼ cup all-purpose flour

¼ cup yellow cornmeal

2 teaspoons granulated sugar

¼ teaspoon baking powder

¼ teaspoon baking soda

⅛ teaspoon salt

¼ cup buttermilk

1 large egg, at room temperature

1 tablespoon honey

1 tablespoon vegetable oil

1. Preheat oven to 350°F and line four cups of a muffin pan with paper liners.

2. In a medium bowl, add flour, cornmeal, sugar, baking powder, baking soda, and salt. Whisk to combine. Set aside.

3. In a small bowl, combine buttermilk, egg, honey, and oil and whisk to combine. Pour wet ingredients into dry ingredients and use a spatula to mix until just combined, about ten strokes. Do not overmix.

4. Divide batter between prepared muffin cups. Bake 18–20 minutes or until muffins spring back when gently pressed in the center and tops are golden brown. Cool in pan 3 minutes, then transfer to a wire rack to cool to room temperature.

Honey Butter Spread

Honey butter is delicious on muffins, corn bread, and biscuits, and it is easy to make! In a small bowl, add 4 tablespoons salted butter at room temperature. Use a hand mixer to cream on low speed until smooth, about 30 seconds. Add 2 tablespoons honey, preferably dark honey, and mix on low speed until smooth, about 30 seconds. Transfer to a serving dish and chill well. Serve at room temperature.

LEMON POPPY SEED MUFFINS

PREP TIME: 10 MIN | COOK TIME: 18 MIN | YIELDS 4 MUFFINS

The bright flavor of lemon plays well with the deeper, earthier flavor of poppy seeds. The glaze, spooned over the muffins once cool, adds an extra layer of tangy lemon flavor, but if you prefer you can replace the lemon juice with ¾ teaspoon milk and ¼ teaspoon vanilla for a milder flavor.

INGREDIENTS

½ cup all-purpose flour

¼ cup granulated sugar

¼ teaspoon baking powder

⅛ teaspoon baking soda

⅛ teaspoon salt

3 tablespoons buttermilk

1 tablespoon plus 1 teaspoon lemon juice, divided

1 large egg, at room temperature

1 tablespoon vegetable oil

1 teaspoon freshly grated lemon zest

¼ teaspoon pure vanilla extract

1 tablespoon poppy seeds

3 tablespoons powdered sugar

1. Preheat oven to 350°F and line four cups of a muffin pan with paper liners.

2. In a medium bowl, add flour, granulated sugar, baking powder, baking soda, and salt. Whisk to combine. Set aside.

3. In a small bowl, combine buttermilk, 1 tablespoon lemon juice, egg, oil, lemon zest, and vanilla. Whisk to combine. Pour wet ingredients into dry ingredients and use a spatula to mix until just combined, about six strokes, then add poppy seeds and fold to combine, four to six strokes. Do not overmix.

4. Divide batter between prepared muffin cups. Bake 18–20 minutes or until muffins spring back when gently pressed in the center and tops are golden brown. Cool in pan 3 minutes, then transfer to a wire rack to cool to room temperature.

5. Once cool, prepare glaze. In a second small bowl, add powdered sugar and remaining 1 teaspoon lemon juice and mix until smooth. Spoon over cooled muffins, then let stand 30 minutes to set before enjoying.

SAVORY CHEDDAR ALE MUFFINS

PREP TIME: 10 MIN | COOK TIME: 18 MIN | YIELDS 4 MUFFINS

These muffins blend the hoppy flavor of beer with the heat of dry mustard and the sharpness of Cheddar cheese to create a deeply savory muffin. Whip up a batch of these muffins for dipping into beer cheese soup, serving alongside roast beef or stew, or just slathering with plenty of salted butter!

INGREDIENTS

½ cup all-purpose flour

¼ teaspoon baking powder

⅛ teaspoon baking soda

⅛ teaspoon dry mustard powder

⅛ teaspoon salt

2 tablespoons ale-style beer

1 large egg, at room temperature

1 tablespoon unsalted butter, melted and cooled

¼ cup shredded sharp Cheddar cheese

1. Preheat oven to 350°F and line four cups of a muffin pan with paper liners.

2. In a medium bowl, add flour, baking powder, baking soda, mustard, and salt. Whisk to combine. Set aside.

3. In a small bowl, combine beer, egg, and butter. Whisk to combine. Pour wet ingredients into dry ingredients and use a spatula to mix until just combined, about six strokes, then add Cheddar cheese and fold to combine, four to six strokes. Do not overmix.

4. Divide batter between prepared muffin cups. Bake 18–20 minutes or until muffins spring back when gently pressed in the center and tops are golden brown. Cool in pan 3 minutes, then transfer to a wire rack to cool to room temperature.

CHERRY ALMOND COFFEE CAKE

PREP TIME: 10 MIN | COOK TIME: 20 MIN | SERVES 1

Cherry and almond are a classic combination, and here they feature in a tender coffee cake. This version uses cherry pie filling layered in the middle of the cake to add a tart yet sweet edge, perfect with coffee. If you do not want to use pie filling you can use frozen tart-sweet cherries that have been thawed and drained.

INGREDIENTS

½ cup all-purpose flour

¼ cup plus 1 tablespoon granulated sugar, divided

¼ teaspoon baking powder

⅛ teaspoon baking soda

⅛ teaspoon ground cinnamon

⅛ teaspoon salt

¼ cup sour cream

1 large egg, at room temperature

1 tablespoon vegetable oil

¼ teaspoon pure vanilla extract

⅛ teaspoon almond extract

¼ cup cherry pie filling

3 tablespoons sliced almonds, divided

1. Preheat oven to 350°F and spray a 5" × 3" mini-loaf pan with nonstick cooking spray.

2. In a medium bowl, add flour, ¼ cup sugar, baking powder, baking soda, cinnamon, and salt. Whisk to combine. Set aside.

3. In a small bowl, combine sour cream, egg, oil, vanilla, and almond extract. Whisk to combine. Pour wet ingredients into dry ingredients and use a spatula to mix until just combined, about six strokes, then add 2 tablespoons almonds and fold to combine, four to six strokes. Do not overmix.

4. Transfer half of batter to prepared pan and top with cherry filling, then cover with remaining batter and top with remaining 1 tablespoon sugar and remaining 1 tablespoon almonds. Bake 20–22 minutes or until bread springs back when gently pressed in the center and top is golden brown. Cool in pan 5 minutes, then transfer to a wire rack to cool to room temperature.

JALAPEÑO CORN MUFFINS

PREP TIME: 10 MIN | COOK TIME: 18 MIN | YIELDS 4 MUFFINS

Pickled jalapeños add a zesty kick to these corn muffins. Pickling reduces the heat in jalapeños, so if you like things extra spicy you can add ⅛ teaspoon cayenne pepper to these muffins to make up for the heat lost during the pickling process.

INGREDIENTS

¼ cup all-purpose flour

¼ cup yellow cornmeal

¼ teaspoon chili powder

¼ teaspoon baking powder

¼ teaspoon baking soda

⅛ teaspoon salt

¼ cup buttermilk

1 large egg, at room temperature

1 tablespoon vegetable oil

2 tablespoons minced pickled jalapeños

1. Preheat oven to 350°F and line four cups of a muffin pan with paper liners.

2. In a medium bowl, add flour, cornmeal, chili powder, baking powder, baking soda, and salt. Whisk to combine. Set aside.

3. In a small bowl, combine buttermilk, egg, and oil and whisk to combine. Pour wet ingredients into dry ingredients and use a spatula to mix until just combined, about six strokes, then add jalapeños and fold to combine, four to six strokes. Do not overmix.

4. Divide batter between prepared muffin cups. Bake 18–20 minutes or until muffins spring back when gently pressed in the center and tops are golden brown. Cool in pan 3 minutes, then transfer to a wire rack to cool to room temperature.

Small-Batch Jalapeño Popper Spread

For an easy spread perfect for these savory muffins, in a medium bowl, combine 1 ounce cream cheese at room temperature, ¼ cup finely shredded Cheddar cheese, 1 tablespoon mayonnaise, 1 tablespoon minced pickled jalapeño, 1 tablespoon crumbled cooked bacon, and ¼ teaspoon taco seasoning. Mix until smooth, then serve immediately or refrigerate up to one week. This is best served at room temperature to make it easier to spread.

BANANA BREAD FOR ONE

PREP TIME: 10 MIN | COOK TIME: 30 MIN | SERVES 1

Banana dessert recipes became popular in the US in the 1930s when banana bread became a standard recipe in many cookbooks. Today banana bread is a staple in coffee shops and bakeries. It is simple, but its simplicity is what helps the banana flavor to shine! For a special flourish, top the unbaked bread with a slice or two of fresh banana before baking.

INGREDIENTS

½ cup all-purpose flour

¼ cup packed dark brown sugar

¼ teaspoon baking powder

¼ teaspoon pumpkin pie spice

⅛ teaspoon baking soda

⅛ teaspoon salt

¼ cup mashed very ripe banana (about ½ medium banana)

2 tablespoons buttermilk

1 large egg, at room temperature

1 tablespoon unsalted butter, melted and cooled

¼ teaspoon pure vanilla extract

1. Preheat oven to 350°F and spray a 5" × 3" mini-loaf pan with nonstick cooking spray.

2. In a medium bowl, add flour, brown sugar, baking powder, pumpkin pie spice, baking soda, and salt. Whisk to combine. Set aside.

3. In a small bowl, combine banana, buttermilk, egg, butter, and vanilla. Whisk to combine. Pour wet ingredients into dry ingredients and use a spatula to mix until just combined, about ten strokes. Do not overmix.

4. Transfer batter to prepared pan. Bake 30–35 minutes or until bread springs back when gently pressed in the center and top is golden brown. Cool in pan 3 minutes, then transfer to a wire rack to cool to room temperature.

BLUEBERRY YOGURT BREAD

PREP TIME: 10 MIN | COOK TIME: 30 MIN | SERVES 1

This version of blueberry coffee cake is the perfect mix of sweet and tangy, thanks to the Greek yogurt. This recipe calls for plain-flavored yogurt, but you can use blueberry yogurt for extra flavor—just reduce the sugar by 2 teaspoons. If you are using frozen berries do not thaw them before folding them into the batter.

INGREDIENTS

½ cup all-purpose flour, divided

¼ cup blueberries

¼ cup granulated sugar

¼ teaspoon baking powder

⅛ teaspoon ground cinnamon

⅛ teaspoon baking soda

⅛ teaspoon salt

¼ cup full-fat plain Greek yogurt

2 tablespoons buttermilk

1 large egg, at room temperature

1 tablespoon vegetable oil

¼ teaspoon pure vanilla extract

⅛ teaspoon almond extract

1. Preheat oven to 350°F and spray a 5" × 3" mini-loaf pan with nonstick cooking spray.

2. In a small bowl, add 1 teaspoon flour and blueberries. Toss gently until blueberries are coated in flour. Set aside.

3. In a medium bowl, add remaining flour, sugar, baking powder, cinnamon, baking soda, and salt. Whisk to combine. Set aside.

4. In a second small bowl, combine yogurt, buttermilk, egg, oil, vanilla, and almond extract. Whisk to combine. Pour wet ingredients into dry ingredients and use a spatula to mix until just combined, about six strokes, then add blueberries and fold to mix, three to four strokes. Do not overmix.

5. Transfer batter to prepared pan. Bake 30–35 minutes or until bread springs back when gently pressed in the center and top is golden brown. Cool in pan 3 minutes, then transfer to a wire rack to cool to room temperature.

Using Yogurt in Baking

Full-fat yogurt can be added to quick breads, muffins, or cakes when you want a soft and tender crumb and a slightly tangy taste. Greek-style yogurt, a strained yogurt that is very thick, can't be swapped 1:1 for milk. It is best to thin it with a little milk or, to retain the full tangy flavor, buttermilk in a ratio of three parts Greek yogurt to one part milk or buttermilk. If you do decide to use a lower-fat yogurt do not use anything less than 2 percent.

CHERRY MUFFINS

PREP TIME: 1¼ HOURS | COOK TIME: 18 MIN | YIELDS 4 MUFFINS

Rehydrating dried fruit before using in recipes for lower-fat baked goods will help to keep your baked items moist. The dried fruit will naturally absorb moisture while baking, and in recipes with less fat, like muffins, you will want to preserve all the moisture you can so your baked goods do not become dry. You can also use orange juice to rehydrate fruit for extra flavor.

INGREDIENTS

¼ cup dried cherries

½ cup boiling water

½ cup plus 2 tablespoons all-purpose flour, divided

¼ cup plus 2 tablespoons granulated sugar, divided

1 tablespoon unsalted butter, chilled

¼ teaspoon baking powder

⅛ teaspoon baking soda

⅛ teaspoon salt

¼ cup whole milk

1 large egg, at room temperature

1 tablespoon vegetable oil

¼ teaspoon pure vanilla extract

1. In a small heat-safe bowl, combine cherries and boiling water. Let stand 1 hour until cherries are soft, then drain. Set aside.

2. Preheat oven to 350°F and line four cups of a muffin pan with paper liners.

3. In a second small bowl, combine 2 tablespoons flour, 2 tablespoons sugar, and butter. Use your fingers to mix until mixture clumps together and is crumbly. Chill until ready to use.

4. In a medium bowl, add remaining ½ cup flour, remaining ¼ cup sugar, baking powder, baking soda, and salt. Whisk to combine. Set aside.

5. In a third small bowl, combine milk, egg, oil, and vanilla and whisk to combine. Pour wet ingredients into dry ingredients and use a spatula to mix until just combined, about six strokes, then add cherries and fold to combine, three to four strokes. Do not overmix.

6. Divide batter between prepared muffin cups. Sprinkle chilled topping evenly over muffins. Bake 18–20 minutes or until muffins spring back when gently pressed in the center and tops are golden brown. Cool in pan 3 minutes, then transfer to a wire rack to cool to room temperature.

CRANBERRY ORANGE MUFFINS

PREP TIME: 1¼ HOURS | COOK TIME: 19 MIN | YIELDS 4 MUFFINS

These muffins are sweet and refreshing, and the textures of crisp topping and chewy fruit make them very special. If you want to have the cranberries more evenly distributed throughout the muffins, you can roughly chop them before soaking them in the orange juice. Feel free to add up to 2 tablespoons chopped pecans if you like.

INGREDIENTS

¼ cup dried cranberries

½ cup orange juice

½ cup plus 2 tablespoons all-purpose flour, divided

¼ cup plus 2 tablespoons granulated sugar, divided

⅛ teaspoon ground cinnamon

1 tablespoon unsalted butter, chilled

¼ teaspoon baking powder

⅛ teaspoon baking soda

⅛ teaspoon salt

¼ cup whole milk

1 large egg, at room temperature

1 tablespoon vegetable oil

½ teaspoon freshly grated orange zest

¼ teaspoon pure vanilla extract

1. In a small microwave-safe bowl, combine cranberries and orange juice. Microwave 1 minute, then let stand 1 hour until cranberries are soft. Drain and set aside.

2. Preheat oven to 350°F and line four cups of a muffin pan with paper liners.

3. In a small bowl, combine 2 tablespoons flour, 2 tablespoons sugar, cinnamon, and butter. Use your fingers to mix until mixture clumps together and is crumbly. Chill until ready to use.

4. In a medium bowl, add remaining ½ cup flour, remaining ¼ cup sugar, baking powder, baking soda, and salt. Whisk to combine. Set aside.

5. In a second small bowl, combine milk, egg, oil, orange zest, and vanilla and whisk to combine. Pour wet ingredients into dry ingredients and use a spatula to mix until just combined, about six strokes. Add cranberries and fold to combine, three to four strokes. Do not overmix.

6. Divide batter between prepared muffin cups. Sprinkle chilled topping evenly over muffins. Bake 18–20 minutes or until muffins spring back when gently pressed in the center and tops are golden brown. Cool in pan 3 minutes, then transfer to a wire rack to cool to room temperature.

COCONUT LIME MUFFINS

PREP TIME: 10 MIN | COOK TIME: 18 MIN | YIELDS 4 MUFFINS

You can use refrigerated coconut milk for this recipe if you have it, but for the best flavor you should use full-fat canned coconut milk. Be sure to shake it well before using, as the fat can separate. Leftover coconut milk can be used in coffee, added to oatmeal, or mixed into smoothies.

INGREDIENTS

½ cup all-purpose flour

¼ cup granulated sugar

¼ teaspoon baking powder

⅛ teaspoon baking soda

⅛ teaspoon salt

3 tablespoons plus 2 teaspoons full-fat canned coconut milk, divided

1 tablespoon plus 1 teaspoon lime juice, divided

1 large egg, at room temperature

1 tablespoon vegetable oil

1 teaspoon freshly grated lime zest

¼ teaspoon pure vanilla extract

¼ cup shredded sweetened coconut

¼ cup powdered sugar

1 tablespoon unsalted butter, melted and cooled

1. Preheat oven to 350°F and line four cups of a muffin pan with paper liners.

2. In a medium bowl, add flour, granulated sugar, baking powder, baking soda, and salt. Whisk to combine. Set aside.

3. In a small bowl, combine 3 tablespoons coconut milk, 1 tablespoon lime juice, egg, oil, lime zest, and vanilla. Whisk to combine. Pour wet ingredients into dry ingredients and use a spatula to mix until just combined, about six strokes, then add shredded coconut and fold to combine, four to six strokes. Do not overmix.

4. Divide batter between prepared muffin cups. Bake 18–20 minutes or until muffins spring back when gently pressed in the center and tops are golden brown. Cool in pan 3 minutes, then transfer to a wire rack to cool to room temperature.

5. In a second small bowl, combine remaining 2 teaspoons coconut milk, remaining 1 teaspoon lime juice, powdered sugar, and butter. Mix until smooth, then spoon over cooled muffins. Let stand 30 minutes so glaze can set.

FRESH PEACH MUFFINS

PREP TIME: 10 MIN | COOK TIME: 18 MIN | YIELDS 4 MUFFINS

If you would like to add more peach flavor to these muffins, you can purée the remaining peach until smooth and use 2 tablespoons of that purée in place of half the buttermilk. Some buttermilk is required to help activate the baking powder, so don't eliminate all of it.

INGREDIENTS

½ cup all-purpose flour

¼ cup packed light brown sugar

¼ teaspoon baking powder

⅛ teaspoon ground cardamom

⅛ teaspoon baking soda

⅛ teaspoon salt

¼ cup buttermilk

1 large egg, at room temperature

1 tablespoon unsalted butter, melted and cooled

1 teaspoon honey

¼ teaspoon pure vanilla extract

⅛ teaspoon almond extract

¼ cup peeled and finely chopped peach (about ⅓ large peach)

1. Preheat oven to 350°F and line four cups of a muffin pan with paper liners.

2. In a medium bowl, add flour, brown sugar, baking powder, cardamom, baking soda, and salt. Whisk to combine. Set aside.

3. In a small bowl, combine buttermilk, egg, butter, honey, vanilla, and almond extract and whisk to combine. Pour wet ingredients into dry ingredients and use a spatula to mix until just combined, about six strokes, then add peach and fold to combine, four to six strokes. Do not overmix.

4. Divide batter between prepared muffin cups. Bake 18–20 minutes or until muffins spring back when gently pressed in the center and tops are golden brown. Cool in pan 3 minutes, then transfer to a wire rack to cool to room temperature.

PUMPKIN BREAD

PREP TIME: 10 MIN | COOK TIME: 30 MIN | SERVES 1

Pumpkin bread is often considered a fall treat; however, most coffee shops and bakeries carry it year-round. Even so, making it at home is quick and simple. Pumpkin purée can easily be frozen, so any purée you have left after making your personal loaf of Pumpkin Bread won't go bad. Freeze leftovers in ¼-cup portions to make future baking easier!

INGREDIENTS

½ cup all-purpose flour

¼ cup packed light brown sugar

¼ teaspoon baking powder

¼ teaspoon pumpkin pie spice

⅛ teaspoon baking soda

⅛ teaspoon salt

¼ cup pumpkin purée

2 tablespoons buttermilk

1 large egg, at room temperature

2 tablespoons vegetable oil

¼ teaspoon pure vanilla extract

1. Preheat oven to 350°F and spray a 5" × 3" mini-loaf pan with nonstick cooking spray.

2. In a medium bowl, add flour, brown sugar, baking powder, pumpkin pie spice, baking soda, and salt. Whisk to combine. Set aside.

3. In a small bowl, combine pumpkin, buttermilk, egg, oil, and vanilla. Whisk to combine. Pour wet ingredients into dry ingredients and use a spatula to mix until just combined, about ten strokes. Do not overmix.

4. Transfer batter to prepared pan. Bake 30–35 minutes or until bread springs back when gently pressed in the center and top is golden brown. Cool in pan 3 minutes, then transfer to a wire rack to cool to room temperature.

Cinnamon Cream Cheese Spread

This simple spread for Pumpkin Bread, or any sweet muffins, can be made from 2 ounces softened cream cheese, 2 tablespoons powdered sugar, 1 tablespoon unsalted butter at room temperature, ¼ teaspoon ground cinnamon, and ¼ teaspoon vanilla extract. Combine all the ingredients in a small bowl and mix until smooth. You can use this spread at once or chill it and use it later. It is best served at room temperature.

PECAN DATE BREAD

PREP TIME: 10 MIN | COOK TIME: 30 MIN | SERVES 1

When shopping for dates it is better to purchase them in the produce department rather than the dried fruit aisle. Dates should be plump to the touch and feel firm but not hard. The skins can be smooth or wrinkled and should be a little glossy. Avoid dates with any crystals of sugar on the outside, as they are not fresh.

INGREDIENTS

⅓ cup all-purpose flour

¼ cup packed light brown sugar

2 tablespoons whole-wheat flour

¼ teaspoon baking powder

¼ teaspoon ground cinnamon

⅛ teaspoon baking soda

⅛ teaspoon salt

1 pinch (about ¹⁄₁₆ teaspoon) ground cardamom

¼ cup buttermilk

2 teaspoons honey

1 large egg, at room temperature

1 tablespoon vegetable oil

¼ teaspoon pure vanilla extract

¼ cup chopped dates

2 tablespoons chopped pecans

1. Preheat oven to 350°F and spray a 5" × 3" mini-loaf pan with nonstick cooking spray.

2. In a medium bowl, add all-purpose flour, brown sugar, whole-wheat flour, baking powder, cinnamon, baking soda, salt, and cardamom. Whisk to combine. Set aside.

3. In a small bowl, combine buttermilk, honey, egg, oil, and vanilla. Whisk to combine. Pour wet ingredients into dry ingredients and use a spatula to mix until just combined, about six strokes. Add dates and pecans and fold to combine, three to four strokes. Do not overmix.

4. Transfer batter to prepared pan. Bake 30–35 minutes or until bread springs back when gently pressed in the center and top is golden brown. Cool in pan 3 minutes, then transfer to a wire rack to cool to room temperature.

CARROT MUFFINS

PREP TIME: 10 MIN | COOK TIME: 18 MIN | YIELDS 4 MUFFINS

These muffins are packed with carrots, pecans, and raisins, and have a flavor and texture similar to carrot cake but with less fat and sugar. For the 3 tablespoons shredded carrot, use a small, peeled carrot and grate it with a fine grater. Don't use ready-grated carrot from the store. It is often dry and less flavorful.

INGREDIENTS

½ cup all-purpose flour

¼ cup packed dark brown sugar

¼ teaspoon baking powder

⅛ teaspoon pumpkin pie spice

⅛ teaspoon baking soda

⅛ teaspoon salt

¼ cup whole milk

1 large egg, at room temperature

1 tablespoon vegetable oil

¼ teaspoon pure vanilla extract

3 tablespoons finely shredded carrot

2 tablespoons chopped pecans

2 tablespoons roughly chopped raisins

1. Preheat oven to 350°F and line four cups of a muffin pan with paper liners.

2. In a medium bowl, add flour, brown sugar, baking powder, pumpkin pie spice, baking soda, and salt. Whisk to combine. Set aside.

3. In a small bowl, combine milk, egg, oil, and vanilla and whisk to combine. Pour wet ingredients into dry ingredients and use a spatula to mix until just combined, about six strokes, then add carrot, pecans, and raisins and fold to combine, four to six strokes. Do not overmix.

4. Divide batter between prepared muffin cups. Bake 18–20 minutes or until muffins spring back when gently pressed in the center and tops are golden brown. Cool in pan 3 minutes, then transfer to a wire rack to cool to room temperature.

CINNAMON SWIRL BREAD

PREP TIME: 10 MIN | COOK TIME: 20 MIN | SERVES 1

While this bread bakes, the cinnamon sugar filling will swirl naturally throughout the small loaf. If you want to add a little texture to this bread, you can add 2 tablespoons chopped almonds or walnuts to the batter along with the cinnamon sugar for a nutty Cinnamon Swirl Bread. You can use all sour cream or all buttermilk, depending on what you have on hand.

INGREDIENTS

½ cup plus 2 tablespoons all-purpose flour, divided

¼ cup plus 3 tablespoons granulated sugar, divided

1 tablespoon unsalted butter, chilled

¼ teaspoon baking powder

⅛ teaspoon baking soda

⅛ teaspoon salt

2 tablespoons sour cream

2 tablespoons buttermilk

1 large egg, at room temperature

1 tablespoon vegetable oil

¼ teaspoon pure vanilla extract

¼ teaspoon ground cinnamon

1. Preheat oven to 350°F and spray a 5" × 3" mini-loaf pan with nonstick cooking spray.

2. In a small bowl, combine 2 tablespoons flour, 2 tablespoons sugar, and butter. Use your fingers to mix until mixture clumps together and is crumbly. Chill until ready to use.

3. In a medium bowl, add remaining ½ cup flour, ¼ cup sugar, baking powder, baking soda, and salt. Whisk to combine. Set aside.

4. In a second small bowl, combine sour cream, buttermilk, egg, oil, and vanilla. Whisk to combine. Pour wet ingredients into dry ingredients and use a spatula to mix until just combined, about ten strokes. Do not overmix.

5. In a third small bowl, combine remaining 1 tablespoon sugar and cinnamon.

6. Transfer half of batter to prepared pan and top with cinnamon sugar mixture, then cover with remaining batter and top with chilled crumble.

7. Bake 20–22 minutes or until bread springs back when gently pressed in the center and top is golden brown. Cool in pan 5 minutes, then transfer to a wire rack to cool to room temperature.

GINGERBREAD CRUMB MUFFINS

PREP TIME: 10 MIN | COOK TIME: 18 MIN | YIELDS 4 MUFFINS

Fresh gingerbread is a popular winter treat in either cake or cookie form. These muffins take all the best flavors of gingerbread cake and make them into a crumble-topped muffin. You can enjoy these warm with a little soft butter or a bit of whipped cream cheese, and a cup of coffee. If you do not have molasses, you can swap it for honey.

INGREDIENTS

½ cup plus 2 tablespoons all-purpose flour, divided

2 tablespoons granulated sugar

¼ teaspoon plus ⅛ teaspoon ground cinnamon, divided

1 tablespoon unsalted butter, chilled

3 tablespoons packed dark brown sugar

¼ teaspoon baking powder

¼ teaspoon ground ginger

⅛ teaspoon baking soda

⅛ teaspoon salt

1 pinch (about ¹⁄₁₆ teaspoon) ground cloves

¼ cup whole milk

1 tablespoon molasses

1 large egg, at room temperature

1 tablespoon vegetable oil

1. Preheat oven to 350°F and line four cups of a muffin pan with paper liners.

2. In a small bowl, combine 2 tablespoons flour, granulated sugar, ⅛ teaspoon cinnamon, and butter. Use your fingers to mix until mixture clumps together and is crumbly. Chill until ready to use.

3. In a medium bowl, add remaining ½ cup flour, remaining ¼ teaspoon cinnamon, brown sugar, baking powder, ginger, baking soda, salt, and cloves. Whisk to combine. Set aside.

4. In a second small bowl, combine milk, molasses, egg, and oil and whisk to combine. Pour wet ingredients into dry ingredients and use a spatula to mix until just combined, about ten strokes. Do not overmix.

5. Divide batter between prepared muffin cups. Sprinkle chilled topping evenly over muffins. Bake 18–20 minutes or until muffins spring back when gently pressed in the center and tops are golden brown. Cool in pan 3 minutes, then transfer to a wire rack to cool to room temperature.

GLAZED LEMON LOAF

PREP TIME: 10 MIN | COOK TIME: 20 MIN | SERVES 1

A little butter mixed into the glaze makes it richer in flavor and gives it a silky texture. You can make this an orange or lime loaf simply by swapping the zest and juice for the citrus fruit you prefer. You could also make a grapefruit loaf, but you should add an extra ½ teaspoon sugar to counter the sourness of the juice.

INGREDIENTS

½ cup all-purpose flour

¼ cup granulated sugar

¼ teaspoon baking powder

⅛ teaspoon baking soda

⅛ teaspoon salt

3 tablespoons buttermilk

1 tablespoon plus 1 teaspoon lemon juice, divided

1 large egg, at room temperature

1 tablespoon vegetable oil

1 teaspoon freshly grated lemon zest

¼ teaspoon pure vanilla extract

¼ cup powdered sugar

1 teaspoon melted unsalted butter

1. Preheat oven to 350°F and spray a 5" × 3" mini-loaf pan with nonstick cooking spray.

2. In a medium bowl, add flour, granulated sugar, baking powder, baking soda, and salt. Whisk to combine. Set aside.

3. In a small bowl, combine buttermilk, 1 tablespoon lemon juice, egg, oil, lemon zest, and vanilla. Whisk to combine. Pour wet ingredients into dry ingredients and use a spatula to mix until just combined, about ten strokes. Do not overmix.

4. Transfer batter to prepared pan. Bake 20–22 minutes or until bread springs back when gently pressed in the center and top is golden brown. Cool in pan 5 minutes, then transfer to a wire rack to cool until just warm.

5. Once loaf is slightly warm, prepare glaze. In a second small bowl, add powdered sugar, melted butter, and remaining 1 teaspoon lemon juice and mix until smooth. Spoon over loaf, letting glaze drip down the sides. Let stand until fully cool before serving.

Oil versus Butter

Ever wondered why a recipe might call for oil instead of butter and whether you could use them interchangeably? The short answer is yes, you can swap them, and your recipe will turn out just fine. Oil is often used to create a more tender, moist crumb in cakes and muffins. Butter adds a richer flavor, but the crumb will be a little firmer when the cake or muffin is cooled.

ZUCCHINI MUFFINS

PREP TIME: 10 MIN | COOK TIME: 18 MIN | YIELDS 4 MUFFINS

Grated zucchini makes these muffins delightfully moist and tender. They are also hearty and make a great breakfast or midday snack. If you want to make this recipe into a loaf, you can use a 5" × 3" mini-loaf pan sprayed with nonstick spray and add an extra 2–3 minutes to the cooking time.

INGREDIENTS

6 tablespoons all-purpose flour

¼ cup granulated sugar

2 tablespoons whole-wheat flour

¼ teaspoon baking powder

⅛ teaspoon ground cinnamon

⅛ teaspoon baking soda

⅛ teaspoon salt

¼ cup whole milk

1 large egg, at room temperature

1 tablespoon vegetable oil

3 tablespoons grated zucchini

2 tablespoons chopped walnuts

1. Preheat oven to 350°F and line four cups of a muffin pan with paper liners.

2. In a medium bowl, add all-purpose flour, granulated sugar, whole-wheat flour, baking powder, cinnamon, baking soda, and salt. Whisk to combine. Set aside.

3. In a small bowl, combine milk, egg, and oil and whisk to combine. Pour wet ingredients into dry ingredients and use a spatula to mix until just combined, about six strokes, then add shredded zucchini and fold to combine, four to six strokes. Do not overmix.

4. Divide batter between prepared muffin cups and sprinkle tops with walnuts. Bake 18–20 minutes or until muffins spring back when gently pressed in the center and tops are golden brown. Cool in pan 3 minutes, then transfer to a wire rack to cool to room temperature.

STRAWBERRY PECAN BREAD

PREP TIME: 10 MIN | **COOK TIME: 30 MIN** | **SERVES 1**

Most strawberry breads have a bright pink color that is boosted by adding a few drops of red food coloring to the batter. This recipe does not include food coloring, so the color of the finished loaf will not be so robustly pink. We eat with our eyes first, and if that pink color will help you enjoy the bread more, feel free to add one drop of red coloring.

INGREDIENTS

½ cup all-purpose flour

¼ cup packed light brown sugar

¼ teaspoon baking powder

⅛ teaspoon baking soda

⅛ teaspoon salt

2 tablespoons buttermilk

2 tablespoons mashed strawberries

1 large egg, at room temperature

1 tablespoon vegetable oil

¼ teaspoon pure vanilla extract

3 tablespoons diced strawberries

2 tablespoons chopped pecans

1. Preheat oven to 350°F and spray a 5" × 3" mini-loaf pan with nonstick cooking spray.

2. In a medium bowl, add flour, brown sugar, baking powder, baking soda, and salt. Whisk to combine. Set aside.

3. In a small bowl, combine buttermilk, mashed strawberries, egg, oil, and vanilla. Whisk to combine. Pour wet ingredients into dry ingredients and use a spatula to mix until just combined, about six strokes, then add diced strawberries and pecans and fold to combine, four to six strokes. Do not overmix.

4. Transfer batter to prepared pan. Bake 30–35 minutes or until bread springs back when gently pressed in the center and top is golden brown. Cool in pan 3 minutes, then transfer to a wire rack to cool to room temperature.

What Is a Stroke?

For muffin and quick bread recipes in this book, the directions say to mix the batter using a specific number of strokes. In this context, a stroke is one turn around the bowl with a spatula. Be sure to pull any dry ingredients from the bottom of the bowl up so each stroke around the bowl is as efficient as possible. The fewer strokes you make, the less gluten you develop, and the more tender the finished result.

DOUBLE CHOCOLATE CHIP BREAD

PREP TIME: 10 MIN | COOK TIME: 30 MIN | SERVES 1

This loaf cake made with Dutch-processed cocoa powder has an earthy, mellow chocolate taste that helps the flavor of the semisweet chips to really pop. You can use regular unsweetened cocoa powder if that is what you have on hand. The flavor will be more robustly chocolatey, which is never a bad thing if you love chocolate.

INGREDIENTS

½ cup all-purpose flour

¼ cup packed light brown sugar

1 tablespoon Dutch-processed cocoa powder

¼ teaspoon baking powder

⅛ teaspoon baking soda

⅛ teaspoon salt

¼ cup buttermilk

1 large egg, at room temperature

1 tablespoon unsalted butter, melted and cooled

¼ teaspoon pure vanilla extract

3 tablespoons semisweet chocolate chips

1. Preheat oven to 350°F and spray a 5" × 3" mini-loaf pan with nonstick cooking spray.

2. In a medium bowl, add flour, brown sugar, cocoa powder, baking powder, baking soda, and salt. Whisk to combine. Set aside.

3. In a small bowl, combine buttermilk, egg, butter, and vanilla. Whisk to combine. Pour wet ingredients into dry ingredients and use a spatula to mix until just combined, about six strokes, then add chocolate chips and fold to combine, four to six strokes. Do not overmix.

4. Transfer batter to prepared pan. Bake 30–35 minutes or until bread springs back when gently pressed in the center and top is golden brown. Cool in pan 3 minutes, then transfer to a wire rack to cool to room temperature.

TOASTED COCONUT BREAD

PREP TIME: 10 MIN | COOK TIME: 35 MIN | SERVES 1

You can toast coconut in large batches and store it in the refrigerator up to a month or in the freezer up to six months. Toasted coconut makes a lovely garnish on cakes and glazed muffins; it can be folded into puddings and custards or added to oatmeal, rice pudding, or bread pudding.

INGREDIENTS

⅓ cup shredded sweetened coconut

½ cup all-purpose flour

¼ cup packed light brown sugar

¼ teaspoon baking powder

⅛ teaspoon baking soda

⅛ teaspoon salt

¼ cup full-fat canned coconut milk

1 large egg, at room temperature

1 tablespoon vegetable oil

¼ teaspoon pure vanilla extract

⅛ teaspoon coconut extract

2 teaspoons powdered sugar

1. Preheat oven to 350°F and spray a 5" × 3" mini-loaf pan with nonstick cooking spray.

2. In a small sauté pan over medium-low heat, add coconut. Cook, stirring constantly, until coconut just turns golden brown, about 5 minutes. Remove pan from heat and cool coconut, stirring constantly for 30 seconds. Set aside.

3. In a medium bowl, add flour, brown sugar, baking powder, baking soda, and salt. Whisk to combine. Set aside.

4. In a small bowl, combine milk, egg, oil, vanilla, and coconut extract. Whisk to combine. Pour wet ingredients into dry ingredients and use a spatula to mix until just combined, about six strokes, then add toasted coconut and fold to combine, four to six strokes. Do not overmix.

5. Transfer batter to prepared pan. Bake 30–35 minutes or until bread springs back when gently pressed in the center and top is golden brown. Cool in pan 3 minutes, then transfer to a wire rack to cool to room temperature. Dust top of loaf with powdered sugar before serving.

PIÑA COLADA BREAD

PREP TIME: 10 MIN | COOK TIME: 30 MIN | SERVES 1

The refreshing combination of coconut, lime, and pineapple echoes the flavor of the popular piña colada cocktail. If you like, you can soak the cake in a little white rum. When the loaf is hot in the pan, poke it with a toothpick twenty times, then spoon over 2 teaspoons of white rum, letting it soak into the holes. Cool in pan completely before you enjoy!

INGREDIENTS

½ cup all-purpose flour

¼ cup granulated sugar

¼ teaspoon baking powder

⅛ teaspoon baking soda

⅛ teaspoon salt

3 tablespoons full-fat canned coconut milk

1 tablespoon lime juice

1 large egg, at room temperature

1 tablespoon vegetable oil

½ teaspoon freshly grated lime zest

¼ teaspoon pure vanilla extract

⅛ teaspoon coconut extract

¼ cup drained crushed pineapple

2 tablespoons shredded sweetened coconut

2 teaspoons powdered sugar

1. Preheat oven to 350°F and spray a 5" × 3" mini-loaf pan with nonstick cooking spray.

2. In a medium bowl, add flour, granulated sugar, baking powder, baking soda, and salt. Whisk to combine. Set aside.

3. In a small bowl, combine milk, lime juice, egg, oil, lime zest, vanilla, and coconut extract. Whisk to combine. Pour wet ingredients into dry ingredients and use a spatula to mix until just combined, about six strokes, then add pineapple and shredded coconut and fold to combine, four to six strokes. Do not overmix.

4. Transfer batter to prepared pan. Bake 30–35 minutes or until bread springs back when gently pressed in the center and top is golden brown. Cool in pan 3 minutes, then transfer to a wire rack to cool to room temperature. Dust top of loaf with powdered sugar before serving.

FRUITCAKE

PREP TIME: 1¼ HOURS | COOK TIME: 35 MIN | SERVES 1

Commercially prepared fruitcakes are often made with dyed candied fruits and have a dense texture. This version replaces candied fruits with dried fruit hydrated in bourbon, then folded into a molasses-flavored batter. If you do not have bourbon, you can use an equal amount of orange juice.

INGREDIENTS

1 tablespoon chopped dried cherries

1 tablespoon chopped golden raisins

1 tablespoon chopped dates

⅓ cup bourbon

½ cup all-purpose flour

¼ cup packed dark brown sugar

¼ teaspoon baking powder

¼ teaspoon ground cinnamon

⅛ teaspoon baking soda

⅛ teaspoon salt

1 pinch (about 1⁄16 teaspoon) ground cloves

¼ cup buttermilk

2 teaspoons molasses

1 large egg, at room temperature

1 tablespoon vegetable oil

¼ teaspoon pure vanilla extract

2 tablespoons chopped walnuts

1. In a small saucepan, add cherries, raisins, dates, and bourbon. Heat over low heat until liquid simmers, about 5 minutes. Turn off heat and let fruit stand 1 hour, then drain and set aside.

2. Preheat oven to 350°F and spray a 5" × 3" mini-loaf pan with nonstick cooking spray.

3. In a medium bowl, add flour, brown sugar, baking powder, cinnamon, baking soda, salt, and cloves. Whisk to combine. Set aside.

4. In a small bowl, combine buttermilk, molasses, egg, oil, and vanilla. Whisk to combine. Pour wet ingredients into dry ingredients and use a spatula to mix until just combined, about six strokes. Add reserved fruit and walnuts and fold to combine, three to four strokes. Do not overmix.

5. Transfer batter to prepared pan. Bake 30–35 minutes or until bread springs back when gently pressed in the center and top is golden brown. Cool in pan 3 minutes, then transfer to a wire rack to cool to room temperature.

GRANOLA MUFFINS

PREP TIME: 10 MIN | COOK TIME: 18 MIN | YIELDS 4 MUFFINS

Granola is a tasty breakfast or snack and so are muffins, so it makes sense to combine them! This recipe makes a handheld granola muffin treat that you can grab on the run or enjoy in a quiet moment. Feel free to use any kind of granola you like, including granola made with dried fruit, nuts, coconut, seeds, and chocolate.

INGREDIENTS

½ cup all-purpose flour

¼ cup granulated sugar

¼ teaspoon baking powder

⅛ teaspoon ground cinnamon

⅛ teaspoon baking soda

⅛ teaspoon salt

¼ cup whole milk

1 large egg, at room temperature

1 tablespoon unsalted butter, melted and cooled

¼ teaspoon pure vanilla extract

⅛ teaspoon almond extract

½ cup granola cereal, divided

1. Preheat oven to 350°F and line four cups of a muffin pan with paper liners.

2. In a medium bowl, add flour, sugar, baking powder, cinnamon, baking soda, and salt. Whisk to combine. Set aside.

3. In a small bowl, combine milk, egg, butter, vanilla, and almond extract and whisk to combine. Pour wet ingredients into dry ingredients and use a spatula to mix until just combined, about six strokes, then add ⅓ cup granola and fold to combine, four to six strokes. Do not overmix.

4. Divide batter between prepared muffin cups and sprinkle remaining granola on top. Bake 18–20 minutes or until muffins spring back when gently pressed in the center and tops are golden brown. Cool in pan 3 minutes, then transfer to a wire rack to cool to room temperature.

CINNAMON CRUNCH MUFFINS

PREP TIME: 10 MIN | COOK TIME: 18 MIN | YIELDS 4 MUFFINS

The crunch in these muffins comes from the crumble topping that is sprinkled on top of the muffins before baking. Be sure to let the topping chill in the refrigerator while you make the muffin batter. If you would like to add 3 tablespoons of finely chopped pecans to this recipe, you can fold them in at the end, and they will add even more texture and flavor.

INGREDIENTS

½ cup plus 2 tablespoons all-purpose flour, divided

¼ cup plus 2 tablespoons granulated sugar, divided

1 tablespoon unsalted butter, chilled

¼ teaspoon baking powder

¼ teaspoon ground cinnamon

⅛ teaspoon baking soda

⅛ teaspoon salt

¼ cup whole milk

1 large egg, at room temperature

1 tablespoon vegetable oil

¼ teaspoon pure vanilla extract

1. Preheat oven to 350°F and line four cups of a muffin pan with paper liners.

2. In a small bowl, combine 2 tablespoons flour, 2 tablespoons sugar, and butter. Use your fingers to mix until mixture clumps together and is crumbly. Chill until ready to use.

3. In a medium bowl, add remaining ½ cup flour, remaining ¼ cup sugar, baking powder, cinnamon, baking soda, and salt. Whisk to combine. Set aside.

4. In a small bowl, combine milk, egg, oil, and vanilla and whisk to combine. Pour wet ingredients into dry ingredients and use a spatula to mix until just combined, about ten strokes. Do not overmix.

5. Divide batter between prepared muffin cups. Sprinkle chilled topping evenly over muffins. Bake 18–20 minutes or until muffins spring back when gently pressed in the center and tops are golden brown. Cool in pan 3 minutes, then transfer to a wire rack to cool to room temperature.

US/METRIC CONVERSION CHARTS

OVEN TEMP CONVERSIONS

Degrees Fahrenheit	Degrees Celsius
200 degrees F	95 degrees C
250 degrees F	120 degrees C
275 degrees F	135 degrees C
300 degrees F	150 degrees C
325 degrees F	160 degrees C
350 degrees F	180 degrees C
375 degrees F	190 degrees C
400 degrees F	205 degrees C
425 degrees F	220 degrees C
450 degrees F	230 degrees C

VOLUME CONVERSIONS

US Volume Measure	Metric Equivalent
⅛ teaspoon	0.5 milliliter
¼ teaspoon	1 milliliter
½ teaspoon	2 milliliters
1 teaspoon	5 milliliters
½ tablespoon	7 milliliters
1 tablespoon (3 teaspoons)	15 milliliters
2 tablespoons (1 fluid ounce)	30 milliliters
¼ cup (4 tablespoons)	60 milliliters
⅓ cup	90 milliliters
½ cup (4 fluid ounces)	125 milliliters
⅔ cup	160 milliliters
¾ cup (6 fluid ounces)	180 milliliters
1 cup (16 tablespoons)	250 milliliters
1 pint (2 cups)	500 milliliters
1 quart (4 cups)	1 liter (about)

WEIGHT CONVERSIONS

US Weight Measure	Metric Equivalent
½ ounce	15 grams
1 ounce	30 grams
2 ounce	60 grams
3 ounce	85 grams
¼ pound (4 ounces)	115 grams
½ pound (8 ounces)	225 grams
¾ pound (12 ounces)	340 grams
1 pound (16 ounces)	454 grams

BAKING PAN SIZES

American	Metric
8 x 1½ inch round baking pan	20 x 4 cm cake tin
9 x 1½ inch round baking pan	23 x 3.5 cm cake tin
11 x 7 x 1½ inch baking pan	28 x 18 x 4 cm baking tin
13 x 9 x 2 inch baking pan	30 x 20 x 5 cm baking tin
2 quart rectangular baking dish	30 x 20 x 3 cm baking tin
15 x 10 x 2 inch baking pan	30 x 25 x 2 cm baking tin (Swiss roll tin)
9 inch pie plate	22 x 4 or 23 x 4 cm pie plate
7 or 8 inch springform pan	18 or 20 cm springform or loose bottom cake tin
9 x 5 x 3 inch loaf pan	23 x 13 x 7 cm or 2 lb narrow loaf or pâté tin
1½ quart casserole	1.5 liter casserole
2 quart casserole	2 liter casserole

HOW TO REDUCE A RECIPE

Original Amount	Half the Amount	One-Third the Amount
1 cup	½ cup	⅓ cup
¾ cup	6 tablespoons	¼ cup
⅔ cup	⅓ cup	3 tablespoons + 1½ teaspoons
½ cup	¼ cup	2 tablespoons + 2 teaspoons
⅓ cup	2 tablespoons + 2 teaspoons	1 tablespoon + 1¼ teaspoons
¼ cup	2 tablespoons	1 tablespoon + 1 teaspoon
1 tablespoon	1½ teaspoons	1 teaspoon
1 teaspoon	½ teaspoon	¼ teaspoon
½ teaspoon	¼ teaspoon	⅛ teaspoon
¼ teaspoon	⅛ teaspoon	dash

INDEX

Note: Page numbers in **bold** indicate recipe category lists and category overviews.

ABOUT THE AUTHOR

Kelly Jaggers is a cookbook author, recipe developer, food photographer, food stylist, and founder of the recipe blog *Evil Shenanigans* (EvilShenanigans .com). She is the author of *The Everything*® *Pie Cookbook, Not-So-Humble Pies, Moufflet, The Everything*® *Easy Asian Cookbook, The Everything*® *Dutch Oven Cookbook, The Everything*® *Easy Instant Pot*® *Cookbook, The Everything*® *Mediterranean Instant Pot*® *Cookbook,* and *The "I Love My Instant Pot*®*" Soup, Stews, and Chilis Recipe Book.* Kelly is also a cooking instructor, personal chef, and caterer. She lives in Dallas with her husband and rescue dogs.

COOKING SOLO
never needs to be boring again!

Pick up or download your copy today!